Ethical
Wisdom

Ethical Wisdom

What Makes Us Good

Mark Matousek

DOUBLEDAY

NEW YORK LONDON TORONTO

SYDNEY AUCKLAND

Copyright © 2011 by Mark Matousek

All rights reserved. Published in the United States by Doubleday,
a division of Random House, Inc., New York, and in Canada by
Random House of Canada Limited, Toronto.

www.doubleday.com

Grateful acknowledgment is made to the following for permission to
reprint previously published material:

Basic Books: Excerpts from *Evil: An Investigation* by Lance Morrow,
copyright © 2004 by Lance Morrow. Reprinted by permission of Basic
Books, a member of the Perseus Books Group.

Henry Holt and Company, LLC: Excerpts from *The Anatomy of
Human Destructiveness* by Erich Fromm, copyright © 1973 by
Erich Fromm. Reprinted by permission of Henry Holt and Company,
LLC.

Jacket design by Michael J. Windsor

LIBRARY OF CONGRESS CATALOGING-IN-PUBLICATION DATA
Matousek, Mark.
Ethical wisdom : what makes us good / by Mark Matousek. —1st ed.
p. cm.
Includes bibliographical references.
1. Values. 2. Conduct of life. I. Title.
BF778.M38 2010
170—dc22
2009031047

ISBN 978-0-385-52789-7

PRINTED IN THE UNITED STATES OF AMERICA

1 2 3 4 5 6 7 8 9 10

First Edition

For Robert Levithan

Contents

Morality, like art,

really does come

down to where

you draw the line.

—OSCAR WILDE

Author's Note

I am deeply indebted to Professor Jonathan Haidt for introducing me to moral foundations theory. Also, as a literary tourist in the hybrid field of moral science, I've relied gratefully on technical data provided by genuine scientists, social and neuroscientific, including Antonio Damasio, Erich Fromm, Dacher Keltner, E. O. Wilson, Frans de Waal, and Philip Zimbardo. Lance Morrow's fascinating book, *Evil: An Investigation,* and Daniel Goleman's hard science reporting (and conversation) also taught me a lot.

Ethical
Wisdom

Introduction

My mother wasn't always a thief. She wasn't really the criminal type. Rebellious, yes—a crook, no—at least not before my father left us. But very good people do bad things sometimes when their luck has run out and nobody's looking.

My deadbeat father skipped town without warning. The shame was worse than the poverty. This was back in the late 1950s, when broken homes weren't common yet, making us pariahs, have-nots, *desgraciados* in our affluent L.A. suburb. My mother had struggled to keep us afloat but could not prevent the humiliation. She wept when the electric company cut our power. She cursed when we lost our car and the phone. She begged the landlord not to evict us when the welfare checks ran out and the five of us were eating matzoh brei—basically, crackers and eggs—on paper plates by candlelight for dinner.

Ida, my mother, was losing it. When a neighbor offered her a job at Super Fair, a weirdly moral-sounding local department store, she jumped at the extra cash and began to work from 4 to 6 a.m., stocking shelves and pricing inventory. My mother slipped out before dawn every morning, while the four of us were still in bed. I can still recall the sound of the screen door slamming, and the strangeness of her new routine. I also remember my sisters becoming less snarky and bitter around that time. After the advent of Super Fair in our lives, mysterious gifts began to appear. Joyce was now wearing brand-new tennis shoes (I noticed because I certainly wasn't). Marcia's battered old purse was replaced by a tangerine-colored item with tassels. Belle, my baby sister, now sported a festive pink snuggly, appliquéd with clowns and balloons. And finally—with what appeared to be fishes-and-loaves magicianship—my mother produced a navy blue coat like the one I had begged for on my birthday, but which was, she had said, beyond our means.

Where did it come from? I wanted to know.

Ida said it had been on "layaway." Now I was positive that she was lying. We had lots of things on layaway—stuff my mother had set aside in stores till she could mange to pay them off, which hadn't happened in quite a while. This coat had never been laid away. This realization—the atrocious fact that my mother was lying—threw a bombshell into my eight-year-old psyche and brought me to the first ethical crossroads of my life. Should I tell her that I knew she was pulling my leg? Or shut my mouth and enjoy the booty? Should I admit to my well-meaning mother that this moral betrayal had robbed me of parental trust? Or should I keep my mouth shut and just be grateful that she had tried to make me happy?

I thanked her for the coat and said nothing. My mother stopped working at Super Fair soon afterward and found a job as a civil servant. After that our family had more money; Ida's thieving career had been flukish and brief. It was a flukishness that paid off in the end, though. My troubled conscience over that purloined coat helped to turn me into a lifelong seeker, someone who questioned truth obsessively. If my mother was a shoplifter what, for instance, did that make me? Could behavior actually be designated evil if it sprang from love? Was I a criminal for accepting her gift? Was it wrong—even sinful, perhaps—to benefit from the fruits of a crime? Or did sin not even *exist*, technically speaking, when no one was around to report it? I felt arrogant, dirty, sorry, and grateful. I also felt deflowered. An ideal had been torn from my budding ethos, forcing me to acknowledge a conflict I was probably too young to face; namely, that the facts of a situation could lead to (at least) two different conclusions *at the same time.* My mother could be a wonderful person who did a cockamamie thing. I could be a thief for saying nothing. My sisters could be accomplices for loving their goodies. All of these things could be true at once. But how was this possible? It all got jumbled up inside me. Thinking about it made me feel sick. It also made me curious.

I became a compulsive seeker. Seekers are peculiar people. We always think there's some mind-blowing truth waiting right outside our field of vision. We're driven by the earnest belief that right, precise questions will open the doors of truth to us. Liberating secrets will be revealed. Seekers are sometimes delusional, but we're also sincerely interested, and like most sincerely compulsive people, our drivenness can lead to wondrous discoveries. This childhood blue coat forced me to wonder—vigorously—about who I was and what constituted right and wrong; how opposite, simultaneous truths could be grokked. This made me reflect on the paradox that where opposites met, wisdom might, indeed, be born if a person learned to hold them in balance. This embracing of contradictory truths, without one canceling out the other, was said by the wise (whose books I began to devour) to be the essence of wisdom itself. My mother was both good and bad; I both loved her and disliked what she'd done; I then repeated variations of her crime on a few occasions, and regretted it afterward. My sisters were co-conspirators who kept their feelings to themselves in the end. All of the things were true.

"Nothing human is foreign to me," said Terence, the Roman philosopher, and he wasn't kidding. We're kaleidoscopes of contradictions, Satyricons of lust, greed, and hatred, rationalizers of fairness and justice, idolaters, cheaters, and fakes—not to mention hypocrites—with hearts that long to be divine. We are moral platypuses with seemingly mismatched parts who manage to come up with healthy eggs. Pulled in opposite directions, we search each day for some sort of middle path, a balance point, to navigate our way through this obstacle course. We ask ourselves the Holy Question: How ought we to live?

Wisdom, in the sense that I mean it, has nothing to do with perfectionism. It doesn't pertain to idealism either, or pretending to be better than we are. "You do not become good by trying to be good, but by finding the goodness that is already within you, allowing that goodness to emerge," a wise man told me. "But it can only emerge if something fundamental shifts in your state of consciousness." That shift is what this book is about.

We are born, each of us, with a moral organ—humankind's crowning glory. "Two things fill the mind with ever increasing wonder and awe," Kant wrote in his *Critique of Practical Reason*. "The starry heavens above me and the moral law within me." This "organ" isn't a literal thing (though its parts literally reside in the brain); it's an innate faculty similar to our human genius for language, mathematics, and art. In the two hundred thousand years since humans branched off from apes to create a new species, this moral organ came into existence to enable our ultrasocial species to live together in relative peace. While it is true that "the world is on fire" with conflict stemming from hatred, anger, and greed, as the Buddha said, it is also true that more acts of kindness, tolerance, forgiveness, and patience transpire on any given day than the mostly bad things that make the paper. "The sum total of goodness vastly outweighs that of meanness," science writer Daniel Goleman told me when we met for an interview. "The ratio between potential and enacted meanness holds at close to zero any day of the year." Although humans inherit a biological bias that permits us to feel anger, jealousy, selfishness, and envy, we inherit an even stronger tendency toward kindness, compassion, cooperation, enthusiasm, nurture, and love, especially toward those in need. In spite of the horrors (and the newsroom shibboleth that "if it bleeds, it leads"), the truth remains that most of us are fundamentally ethical most of the time in most of the ways that truly matter.

For carnivorous primates, this is nothing short of a miracle. Wisdom-wise, humans are works in progress. Still, this moral organ's potential will impress even the most pessimistic. Your greatest surprise may be to learn that it is primarily emotions that enable morality. Contrary to what we've been taught in a left-brained, logic-obsessed culture, emotions, not reason, are the bedrock of ethical life; without them, the most rational human being cannot be empathic or morally sound. You'll learn that our ethical lives are dictated by complex, moment-to-moment interactions between the most ancient part of the brain—the limbic system that houses emotion—and the most recently evolved part, the neocortex, where reason, language, and analysis are created. The neocortex is also where the moral imagination—our ability to step outside of ourselves and into the feelings of others—takes place. The understanding of what it means to suffer not only our own pain, which anything with a rudimentary nervous system can do, but also the pain of others, has long been considered the distilled essence of our humanity. Altruism, which comes from the Latin root *alter*, or "other," could not exist without this distinction.

Our moral organ has five primary foundations. Similar to our language faculty, which enables us to learn parts of speech—

juggling nouns, adjectives, and verbs into sentences that mean something greater than each word alone—and may even be beautiful—the moral faculty derives wisdom, as well as meaning, from its own quintet of values. These universal moral foundations appear to have remained the same throughout recorded history according to psychologist Jonathan Haidt, who first popularized this theory. From the Kung bushmen to a Boise soccer mom to a Japanese stock trader pounding the pavement, they are universal:

- First, we're concerned with *harm and care.* As "communitarians under the skin" who survive through interconnection, and dislike seeing or feeling the pain of others, we have especially keen moral emotions related to threat as well as nurturing. This foundation underlies kindness and all forms of emotional and physical succor and protection.
- Second, we're devoted to *justice and fairness*—the rules of reciprocity, autonomy, reputation management, revenge, and punishment that enable us to live as individuals in groups. This foundation generates laws and rights and depends on an underlying, unavoidable, sometimes self-centered belief in just deserts.
- Third, we depend on *in-group loyalty* for our survival. This foundation engenders patriotism, tribal pride, and self-sacrifice for the community; it's also why we automatically treat out-group members differently than our personal cohorts, *and always worse.* Loyalty is crucial to ethics, but in-group favoritism is also our nemesis as it underlies tribal conflict, war, and aggression.
- Fourth, we care about *authority and respect.* As hierarchical animals with pecking orders to consider, we have a strong, instinctive attraction toward leadership and the respect of elders, as well as a reverence for tradition. This foundation

is both an enormous help, as when "good" authority figures lead us to higher ground, and a moral hazard, as when power mongers dupe us with charisma or we allow ourselves to forgo ethics in favor of obedience to questionable people or causes.

- Fifth, we have an innate, elevating need for *purity and sacredness.* This foundation, rooted in our central moral emotion— disgust—turns us from animality toward the divine, and explains our perennial taste for religion (of which some forty thousand have been created to date). Like the four other moral receptors, this hunger for purity can be abused when an individual, nation, or faith plays on our disgust reflex by portraying enemies as morally impure, as in the case of anti-Semites and homophobes.

As we get to know this moral organ, it's helpful to remember that the first two foundations—harm/care and justice/fairness— concern themselves with the protection of *individuals,* while the three others serve the purpose of binding the *group* together.

In the same way that, as toddlers, our aptitude for language allowed for verbal acquisition before we determined how we would use it, or what particular language we would speak, so our universal moral grammar predisposes us to ethical choices without our full knowledge or understanding of what those choices will be. While the five innate principles I just described guide our moral judgments, they are largely inaccessible to conscious awareness. Having a strong moral reaction and being unable to rationally explain that reaction is what Haidt calls "moral dumbfounding"—further proof that emotions, and not reason, shape our moral impulses. Let's say that a woman is cleaning out her closet and finds an old American flag. She doesn't want the flag anymore, so she cuts it up into pieces and uses the rags to clean her bathroom. Does that feel wrong to you? If so, why? How about eating the family kitten that was run over by a car in front of your house? You've heard that cat meat is an epicurean delight in China; why not whip up some pussy lo mein? Most of us are disgusted by these suggestions—we find them wrong, unsavory, obnoxious. But *why* do we feel this way, exactly? Reaching inside for rational answers, we find nothing but feelings posing as facts. This is how moral dumbfounding works.

To make ethical life even more of a breeze, these five foundations—hardwired inside our skulls when mastodons still pounded the earth—depend largely on perceptions that have little to do with the actual situation at hand. Our moral choices depend on what we *think* or *feel* has happened, not on what really occurred. Interpretation is everything. The moral sense is just as prone to illusion as the rest of our senses, easily misled by filters ranging from language (think of euphemisms) to appearance (think of sheep's clothing), to imaginative gymnastics of innumerable, self-deceiving kinds. To function properly, the moral faculty must interface accurately with other mental capacities—memory, attention, language, vision, emotion, and beliefs. Because it relies on specialized brain systems, damage to these systems can lead to deficits in moral judgment. When the brain is compromised, from birth or through accident, ethical ability suffers proportionately.

No two people make identical ethical choices because no two brains are exactly alike. We know this because the past twenty years have been a watershed time for neurology. Functional magnetic resonance imaging (fMRI) has enabled us, for the first time in history, to study the human body *in the act of feeling*—the moral science equivalent to putting a foot on the moon. This has given us a laser-beam look into how our ethical choices are made. Thanks to the fMRI machine, we now know that many of our behaviors, even morally loaded ones like altruism and rudeness (previously believed to be under our conscious control), are caused by unconscious automatic physiological responses. What's more, we know that people can't really stop themselves from making up post hoc explanations for whatever it is they've just done for unconscious reasons. Fallible though we may be, however, we're not just apes with better hairdos. Homo sapiens are superior moral beings altogether, and here are the gamma waves to prove it.

Based on findings in evolutionary biology, cognitive psychology, anthropology, economics, linguistics, and neurobiology, we're reaching a level of self-transparency beyond our wildest imaginings. Crucial blind spots are being illuminated, including why we allow ourselves to cheat, but just so much; why we overestimate our virtue and underestimate the power of situations to bring out our Mr. Hyde; why, as the Germans say, "When the penis gets hard the mind goes soft"; why residents of flat places like Texas tend to be conservatives while individuals who live near water tend to be liberal; how men and women differ morally; why children are such good con artists; why non-abstinent, right-wing Christian teenagers are less likely than atheists to wear condoms during sex; and why we're so hopeless at predicting what will make us happy. These and myriad other riddles are being solved by neurologists and psychologists.

Two discoveries, in particular, are amping up this revolution in moral science. The first is "neuroplasticity," the discovery that our brains and behavior can be resculpted with practice. Once believed to be isolated lumps of gray matter cogitating between our ears, our brains turn out to be more like interloping Wi-Fi octopuses with invisible tentacles slithering in many directions at all times, constantly picking up messages we're not aware of and prompting reactions in ways never before understood. Contrary to the old wives' tale that humans are born with a fixed number of brain cells that only diminish over time, our bodies produce *one hundred thousand* new brain cells every day until we die. This has radically altered how psychologists think about personal change. While much of our behavior is hardwired from birth and ratified by the culture we live in, there's far more room for resculpture through practice than the old leopard-and-its-spots cliché would have us believe.

The second great boon has come with the discovery of mirror neurons. In 1995, a neuroscientist at the University of Parma, Giacomo Rizzolatti, identified the mechanism whereby empathy (and a host of other behaviors) is communicated *physiologically*. The sole purpose of mirror neurons is to reflect what we see in the world around us and imitate it, instantly—literally "bringing the outside inside"—in order to harmonize with our environments. These "empathy neurons" (or "Dalai Lama neurons" as one brain scientist calls them) match up our inner reality with the world around us, helping to dissolve the barrier between self and other (the goal of most wisdom traditions, coincidentally). In order to know other people, nature provided us with a mechanism for *becoming* other people—at least a little bit. This does not happen deliberately; mirror neurons are a subconscious, body-to-body communication network that makes social life possible. They help to undergird moral behavior first learned in our infancy, smiling when our mother smiles, absorbing empathic tendencies from the way our parents care for us. Have you ever wondered why seeing a yawn makes you yawn too, or witnessing someone weeping automatically brings a tear to your eye? Mirror neurons are the answer. They are our primary physical means of stepping outside our own skin.

Humans share a need for self-transcendence. Wisdom traditions agree on this point as well. Our moral organ helps us to escape the hell of self-centeredness by learning to bridge opposing truths— our needs and those of others—thus becoming "bigger" people. Psychologist Peter Singer refers to this self-extension as "expanding the circle." This call for empathic expansion has never been more urgent. We wince at images of our own greed—the polar bear stranded on a sheet of ice no bigger than a Winnebago. We're disgusted by our own moral failings and recognize the need to dispel them. In the years since 9/11, with industrial waste from China blanketing the western coast of California and nuclear weapons in Pakistan, nothing seems more important than this circular expansion. With the decoding of the human genome, our species has become capable of enormous good, such as curing diseases, as well as great potential evil, as with human cloning. Since uncovering many of nature's hitherto secret blueprints, we've become "increasingly important subcontractors in the work of Creation," Lance Morrow writes, assuming greater and greater responsibility for good and evil in the world. As one scientist suggested to me, in fact, "At some time in the future, we will have to decide how human we wish to remain."

We know how paradoxical we can be, how wayward, selfish, and blinded by passion; how easily our reasoning minds can dupe us. We know that we are, indeed, "predictably irrational," as behavioral economist Dan Ariely writes, and we are well aware of how hopeless we can be at foretelling the outcomes of our own oddball choices and self-contradictions. Americans have watched our national level of well-being sink by half in the past fifty years. It hardly seems accidental that moral science is exploding simultaneously with global endangerment and declining happiness stats. There's a tick-tocking urgency behind this coincidence, a perfect storm of destructive and instructive forces assaulting our moral consciousness. Alongside our deepening knowledge of what makes us good is an increasing awareness of what makes us monstrous. We know that while goodness may be universal, it is also fragile. We're all too aware that while empathy can be easily aroused, it can also be quickly forgotten. "Human goodness appears when we least expect it, under conditions that are little understood and difficult to create," we're reminded by psychologists Anne Colby and William Damon. "It can arise in settings that seem devoid of anything but sheer evil [and] vanish in the midst of fortune and happy companionship." Political scientist James Q. Wilson expresses this even more bitingly: "We are softened by the sight of one hungry child, but hardened by the sight of thousands."

This is not because we're secretly malevolent. Human contradictions have nothing to do with original sin or the presence of some corrupting, unkillable serpent slithering through the garden of virtue. This is an essential point. Western culture has bequeathed to us a fairly horrendous image of our inherent nature. Sigmund Freud, who almost single-handedly defined the psyche for a majority of people in the West, made declarations about humanity that are enough to put anybody on Prozac. "I have found little that is good about human beings on the whole," complained our first scientist of the mind. "In my experience, most of them are trash." I beg your pardon? People care about their brethren, Freud actually believed, "in order to gratify their aggressiveness, to exploit [their neighbor's] capacity for work without recompense, to use him sexually without his consent, to seize his possessions, to humiliate him, to cause him pain, to torture and to kill him." No kidding?

When the notion of the "selfish gene" was misappropriated from a book about biology, this downcast view appeared to be backed up by the discovery that our chromosomes themselves were inherently vicious. Scientists have been trying to set the record straight ever since. "Evolution is a process that systematically favors selfishness," one biologist wrote. "*But evolutionary theorists define selfishness in significantly different ways from people who make moral attributions* [italics mine]. There is no necessary connection between psychological and genetic forms of selfishness." Please read those sentences twice. "Those who see fit to maximize their profit and pleasure at the expense of others may well fail to propagate their genes," this scientist continued. "On the other side of this coin, those who are willing to sacrifice their interests for the sake of others . . .

may well propagate more of their genes than those who are not." In spite of such expert protestations, there's been a widespread, perverse refusal to acknowledge what Richard Dawkins (who coined the phrase "selfish gene") actually meant. Frans de Waal, one such critic of the evil-gene school, compared this irrational belief to imagining a species of meat-eating animals who've managed to trick themselves out of a taste for flesh. How could humanity have "unearthed the will and strength to defeat the forces of its own nature," asked de Waal, or duped itself into being something it wasn't, "like a shoal of piranhas that decides to turn vegetarian?" The misanthropes didn't have much of a clue.

There's been a widespread, superstitious fear in our culture that if we were to err too far on the side of self-approval—as a general way of seeing ourselves—the species would tip irreversibly into the wanton abyss. "Never forget"—the slogan of those who fear that the Holocaust will be repeated if we glance away from its memory—becomes, all too easily, "never forgive." This is the danger of negative focus; it fulfills self-prophetically. Any therapist worth his hundred bucks, even a Freudian, will tell you that healing and wisdom come from locating our *strengths* and building upon them. This is not a denial of evil. It's just a smarter approach to promoting goodness, considering how the brain works. Ralph Waldo Emerson, America's first self-help author, was saying this back in the 1880s. "Do not waste yourself in rejection, nor bark against the bad, but chant the beauty of the good," wrote the author of "Self-Reliance." Sholem Asch, the Jewish writer, agreed: "It is of the highest importance not only to record and recount, both for ourselves and for the future, the evidences of human degradation, but side by side with them to set forth evidences of human exaltation and nobility. Let the epic of heroic deeds of love, as opposed by those of hatred, of rescue as opposed to destruction, bear equal witness to unborn generations." Since our brains are wired to learn through suggestion, mirroring, repetition, and guidance—not self-hatred—"elevation" (a newly identified emotion that we will explore at length later) is a more effective path for encouraging positive self-awareness.

The positive psychology movement, begun by Martin Seligman in the late 1980s, was seminal in shifting public discourse from what's wrong with us to what's right. This movement has provided a much-needed counterbalance to the overpathologized, half-empty-glass refrain of a narcissistic culture obsessed with its own darkness. Seligman argued that psychology had lost its way; that the mental health field had become obsessed with the dark side of human nature and blinded us to what was good, noble, brave, even occasionally selfless, in ourselves. Doctors had the DSM (*Diagnostic and Statistical Manual*) to define our maladies, but psychologists didn't even have a language with which to talk about the upper reaches of our psychology. Years of research helped Seligman create a diagnostic list of six human character virtues—wisdom, courage, humanity, justice, temperance, and transcendence—as well as three dozen sub-traits (the idea that temperance includes forgiveness, humility, prudence, and self-regulation, for example). Our ethical bag of goodies began to open, including the self-transcending emotions of wonder and awe.

Elevation—the emotion of being uplifted—explains a lot about why our species has thrived in spite of extreme destructiveness. This is a fascinating point. If it weren't for the power of elevation, Barack Obama would not be in the White House. Grassroots movements in general would lose their power to prevail against the odds. Positive psychology has shown us that humans gravitate toward the good and the hopeful. The truth convinces us most of the time. We're magnetized, as a species, by beauty. Indeed, goodness, truth, and beauty form a golden triangle of human ideals—the things that make life worth living. In the presence of beauty, goodness, and truth, we find ourselves illuminated, connected to something larger than ourselves. In the words of Descartes, "This great light in the intellect generates a great propensity in the will." This is because "the brain is preset for kindness," as Daniel Goleman tells me. We are rewarded, inwardly, by loving; it's different from feeling aversive in the world. We aspire to be better people not for some abstract reason but because we long for a good life and the wisdom to enjoy it. A good life is one based on self-understanding, which leads to deeper connection to others, which leads to dedication to something greater than (but not excluding) individual happiness. "An ethical life is one in which we identify ourselves with other, larger, goals, thereby giving meaning to our lives," Seligman insisted when we spoke. Not only do less selfish people tend to be happier, they also live longer and have better physical health than their self-centered counterparts.

This book will show you how and why. While we are certainly ethical creatures in progress, and struggle daily to bridge selfishness with compassion, our native inclination—"the herd instinct in the individual," as Nietzsche called it—falls decisively on the side of connection. Good people—meaning the vast majority of us who do as little harm to others as possible—not only live longer but leave more offspring. This process, repeated through thousands of generations, is what pumped our neocortex to such freakishly large proportions. Evolution has proved, incontestably, that "a group of cooperative altruists will outcompete a group of selfish cheaters," as moral psychologist Marc Hauser writes. This is why values such as honor, altruism, justice, compassion, and mercy have come to define human aspiration. The Greeks had a word for such aspiration—*arete*—meaning excellence, virtue, or goodness, especially of a functional sort. "The *arete* of a knife is to cut well. The *arete* of an eye is to see well. The *arete* of a person is goodness," explains Jonathan Haidt.

Not perfection. Morality, like all things human, will always remain an inexact science, a probability game based on certain fixed features but open to enormous variation. People are not integers, after all; test tubes, graphs, and machines will never reduce us to less than what we are. No scientist will ever predict infallibly the behavior of all future humans. This has nothing to do with metaphysics, but instead points to our learning curve as a species. We use only a fraction of our brain's capacity, less than 20 percent, to be generous, and it seems likely that we access only a modest percentage of our moral gifts as well. It may even be possible that as-yet-undiscovered powers exist in us that drive ethical life as much as neurons. This mysterious aspect of human life needs to be factored in; otherwise, we risk losing our humanity in the process of understanding it, by reducing ourselves to proteins, synapses, and protoplasm. Anyone who has witnessed the inexplicable way in which physically disabled people seem spiritually enlarged even as their bodies decline, for instance, will understand my meaning here. "There's a part of us that is not bound by our physical circumstances," a pediatrician who works with cancer patients told me, "that actually grows in direct proportion to what we lose." We are more than our bodies, in other words, more even than the sum of our minds, and we cannot explore the nature of goodness without a chink left open for the unknown. Despite academic efforts to play down this mystery, we cannot make it go away or twist the elusive parts of ourselves into concrete, empirical info-bytes.

WHAT THIS BOOK IS NOT

A few provisos before we're off. Ethics is a minefield of opposing ideologies, special interests, and temperamental proclivities made explosive by the importance of the topic. Perhaps more than any area of inquiry aside from faith, the moral realm is open to high dudgeon, defensiveness, and subjective interpretation; despite shared universal tendencies, this subject retains its fascination precisely because no two people—much less two groups—will ever agree on everything. To keep our focus on what really matters for ethical wisdom to improve our lives, I've deliberately avoided the most cliché, hot-button topics. I've also avoided any discussion of good and evil as interpreted by the major religions; the reader will find little mention of Satan, hell, heaven, redemption, or sin (in its gospel sense) here. There will be no in-depth philosophical analysis of virtue, or the fascinating evolution of this shifting concept throughout history. I've avoided the academic hornet's nest as well—where eggheads could argue the dust off a butterfly's wing—and put aside conflicting political considerations. By keeping my nose out of religion, academia, and politics, my hope has been to create a secular, dogma-free, prejudice-free, politically incorrect overview of what we know about our innate ethical sense, with as little cultural quibbling as possible. Political distinctions have been made only when they point to more general principles, or are particularly interesting. We learn in Part Three, for example, that the Dutch dislike aristocracy because their low-lying terrain is subject to flooding, and the rich (who have a historic dislike for getting their hands dirty) tend not to pitch in to help the community. This is neither a condemnation of the rich nor an argument for Marxism. It's an illustration of the unbreakable link between social customs and community survival, a connection with sometimes bizarre manifestations (the Ik people of East Africa will make you gag). Finally, the book's structure is purely idiosyncratic and unscientific, an amateur's reimagining of moral foundations theory in an ascending spiral of concern, from care to purity. None of these five foundations is distinct; they constantly overlap and converge in our everyday ethical lives. The material is arranged in the way that it is for narrative enjoyment alone.

As the first generation to call ourselves global, we stand at a moral crossroads. Luckily, our brain has provided us with higher angels to meet this challenge. Evolution is "thrifty and tinkering," after all, as neurologist Antonio Damasio writes in *Descartes' Error,* and may well be pushing our complex species toward a more benevolent future, in spite of what we read in the paper. This book is a mirror on that path.

The Laugh That Preceded Philosophy

[HARM/CARE]

Part One

Man is the primate that emerged at the point of
evolution where instinctive determination had
reached a minimum and the development of the
brain a maximum. The combination of minimal
instinctive determination and maximal brain
development had never occurred before in animal
evolution and constitutes, biologically speaking,
a completely new phenomenon.

—ERICH FROMM

Homo Duplex

O N THE AFTERNOON OF JULY 7, 1999, Dr. Emmanuel
Mahfouz, a third-year medical student at the University
of Texas Health Science Center, was called to the hospital emergency
room to diagnose a bizarre case. The patient, a slender thirty-five-
year-old Guatemalan named Juan, had been experiencing bizarre
mood swings for the past two months. Disheveled, wild-eyed, and
scowling, Juan sat on a bed in the examining room, looking psy-
chotic, while his overwrought wife explained to the team the
sequence of events that had led them there.

"This poor woman!" Mahfouz tells me. He's a diminutive
Egyptian fellow with an effervescent demeanor and huge ears.
"She'd watched this Jekyll and Hyde thing happen to him," the doctor remembers. "In the past two months, her husband had turned
into somebody else. He was belligerent, antagonistic, and uncooper-
ative." Juan had begun having violent outbursts that forced him to
take a leave of absence from his job. Sitting on the bed in the ER that
day, he looked like an animal trapped in a corner, ready to burst with
rage.

"It was the strangest thing I'd ever seen," Mahfouz tells me. "My team and I were completely stumped. The patient seemed neurologically intact—what we call 'alert and oriented times three.' This is when a person can tell you the date, place, and who they are. Then Juan would just sit there giving us the evil eye. He cursed one of the nurses in Spanish. We sent him for an MRI."

The results shocked everyone who saw them. "This man's brain was riddled with holes," says Mahfouz. In the left frontal lobe of Juan's brain—the area responsible for executive skills, emotional control, and decision making—the team found a cyst the size of a walnut, filled with a common "neurological worm" that enters the body through undercooked pork. Although such parasites live inside us much of the time, Mahfouz explains, they lie dormant. Sometimes the worm larvae mature, however, wreaking neurological havoc as they had in Juan's brain. The doctor shows me the photograph of a worm-ridden brain in a textbook. It looks like a striated, circular slice of Jarlsberg cheese.

"The cyst was enormous and filled with worms," he says. Juan was rushed into the OR, where Mahfouz and his colleagues performed a craniotomy to remove the vermin. The surgery took seven hours, but when it was over and the patient had woken up in the recovery room, his personality had returned to normal. "It was amazing!" this physician remembers. "This guy was back to his old self, just like that. He had no idea that he'd been acting so weird. His wife was so relieved! If I hadn't seen it with my own eyes, I wouldn't have thought this was possible."

How is it possible that an undercooked taco can turn a good man into a tyrant? To understand this, we need to take a brief tour through the human brain.

The three-pound human brain, with its sixty miles of neural wiring, is composed of three basic structures, which have evolved from bottom to top. First there's the brain stem, whose basic architecture we share with all mammals. This innermost core of the brain runs the autonomic nervous system, which includes involuntary functions like breathing, heart rate, and digestion. Atop the brain stem is the midbrain, hardware we share with other primates, which houses the limbic system (also known as the reptile brain), where our most primitive, fight-or-flight emotions begin.

Finally, crowning them both is the neocortex, which only humans have. This most recent evolutionary addition gives us our higher function: the ability to think linearly, as in complex language, as well as to formulate abstract, symbolic systems, as we do in mathematics. Our neocortex allows for the subtlety of emotional life, the ability to have feelings *about* our feelings. While the midbrain's emotional system is ancient, automatic, and very fast, the reasoning system of the neocortex is newer, slower, and motivationally weaker (if you've ever tried talking yourself out of a strong feeling, you know that this is true). The cortex is both our greatest gift and, as you'd expect from a new gadget, the place where most things can go wrong.

This brilliant, problematic cortex is divided into two hemispheres. To greatly oversimplify, the right hemisphere is the seat of intuition, moral emotion, and connection to others (feeling), while the left hemisphere controls reason, language, and individuation (thinking). Our right brain draws much of its information from the physical senses, while our left brain takes most of its cues from mental images. One part of us is born seeing the forest, in other words, so the other part can see the trees. We've known this since the late eighteenth century, when French anatomist Meinard Simon du Pui introduced the notion of *Homo duplex*. It was then we began to understand that our brain's two hemispheres actually house two distinct kinds of mind. Connected by the corpus callosum (from the Latin for "great bridge"), these two sides of the brain work together in such perfect harmony that we're unaware most of the time that "man is not one, but two," as Robert Louis Stevenson described it in his story about Dr. Jekyll and Mr. Hyde. Not until the cortex is disabled or damaged do we realize how schizoid our brains really are and how quickly what we call "identity" can be made to dissolve, taking with it moral thinking.

The famous case of Phineas Gage revealed this strange fact for the first time. One September afternoon in 1848, Gage, an employee for the Rutland and Burlington Railroad, was commandeering a railroad construction crew just outside Cavendish, Vermont. Self-assured and well liked—Antonio Damasio likens him to Jimmy Cagney in his book *Descartes' Error*—Phineas was lighting a match while working near combustible material, became distracted for a moment, and caused an enormous blowout. "The explosion is so brutal that the entire gang freezes," as Damasio tells it. "There's a whistling sound as if a rocket was fired at the sky." A thirteen-pound iron rod had entered Gage's left cheek, pierced the base of his skull, and traversed the front of his brain, exiting at high speed through the top of his head. "The rod lands more than a hundred feet away, covered in blood and brains," recounts Damasio. "Phineas Gage has been thrown to the ground. He is stunned, silent, but awake."

Miraculously, Gage survived. The accident destroyed not only the sight in his right eye but also something far more important and enigmatic. With the puncturing of his frontal lobe, Gage lost his character. Damasio describes the change: "The equilibrium ... between his intellectual faculty and animal propensities" had been destroyed. Where he had been amiable and easy to work with, Gage was now "fitful, irreverent, indulging at times in the grossest profanity which was not previously his custom, manifesting but little deference for his fellows, impatient of restraint or advice when it conflicts with his desires, at times pertinaciously obstinate, yet capricious and vacillating, devising many plans of future operation, which are no sooner arranged than they are abandoned . . . a child in his intellectual capacity and manifestations, he [has] . . . the animal passions of a strong man."

In the centuries since Gage's accident, his story has become to neuroanatomists what Ben Franklin's key in the lightning storm was to physicists. Gage's brain, studied by the finest scientific minds of his day, revealed secrets about our complex moral nature never before imagined. While science already understood the brain to be the foundation for language, perception, and motor function, Gage's case revealed the existence of systems in the brain dedicated to the social dimensions of reasoning. This was big news. The notion that preciously acquired social skills and ethical rules could be lost was a shocker. Ethics were absent in Gage after the accident, in spite of the fact that many other parts of his intelligence— memory, language, and perception—remained intact. He became overtly self-sabotaging and unable to care about his own survival. He alienated and abandoned a family he had once loved. The disassociation ruined him, lost him friends and supporters, and rendered him unemployable in any meaningful sense. After traveling around the country in a freak-show circus, Phineas Gage died penniless and epileptic at the age of thirty-eight.

NATURE FIRST

Gage's accident reveals the disturbing fact that what we call character can be stolen from us by stimulating or disengaging a corresponding part of the brain. Read that sentence twice; it may be the single hardest thing for you to swallow in this book. When the hypothalamuses of rats are stimulated with electric current, the animals can become ferocious, hypersexual, or gluttonous. Remind you of anyone at the mall? When researchers in Zurich passed strong magnets over the right prefrontal cortexes of lab subjects, they found that things like trust, care, harm, and fair dealing can be made to "fade away like radio noise subsumed by static," according to science reporter Robert Lee Hotz. This too-intimate link of morality to the physical body, as in Phineas Gage's case, is threatening to our sense of self. Just as we resist the notion that emotions are the foundation of ethical life, we bristle at the idea that morality is determined by nature first and nurture second. We resist the idea of biological explanations for our higher cortical functions, as E. O. Wilson told me in his office at Harvard one afternoon. The creature responsible for *cogito ergo sum*—nature-fearing, death-fearing humans—has never been quite comfortable with his animal nature. We have preferred to see ourselves as tabulae rasae—empty canvases to be etched and highlighted by family and culture—not genetically programmed like our orangutan cousins.

"We've never liked that much," Wilson says with a chuckle, meaning humanity's furry past. As the founder of sociobiology— whose central tenet is that social behavior in animals is genetically founded—Wilson, a myrmecologist by training (he studies ants), was scorned and reviled after suggesting thirty years ago that human social behavior is preprogrammed, at least in part. Observing the mating patterns, territorial fights, pack hunting, and hive society of social insects, Wilson and his colleagues were led to believe that the key link between the social and natural sciences was not the study of higher reason but rather emotion, and the emotional centers of the brain. While genes did not fully dictate behavior, they were key prognosticators in moral life.

Before Wilson came along, adaptationist thinking about physiological mechanisms such as the heart, lungs, and immune system was common in evolutionary biology. But the discovery that our psychological oddities were cut from the same genetic cloth was revolutionary. Suddenly, in addition to brain centers for sight, sound, taste, and so on, there were, sociobiologists discovered, language modules, incest modules, models for cheater detection, sex preferences, foraging (what we'd call shopping), alliance tracking, and so on. Over the course of eons, some modules were chosen as being more "fit" for their environment in the Darwinian process of selection. What was "good," meaning most optimally fit for survival and reproduction in a particular environment, became defined over time; and since natural selection is creative, it could sprout new behaviors in response to shifting demands around us, fine-tuning traits like altruism, loyalty, and so on. Contrary to what we've been taught, our behavior is inseparable from nature, just as reason is inseparable from emotion. Our humanness depends on animal wisdom, the grunt—and smile and frown and laughter—that preceded philosophy.

Knowing the role that nature plays in the formation of moral life, we're now free to ask: What about nurture?

Mirrors in the Mind

Virtually from the time we're born, our primitive, premoral responses are already dividing our baby world in half—between what we want and what we don't. Infants perceive the "goodness" of the world around them in terms of getting what they crave. Those objects that satisfy the baby's desire are seen as good and just, while unsatisfying stimuli are seen as bad and unfair. Anger is the infant's automatic response to not getting what it wants, its first raised fist against cosmic injustice. Child psychologist and ethologist William Charlesworth has suggested that "a baby's protests against the withdrawal of maternal care may be its first expression of moral outrage," its first experience of the world being an unfair place where things that *ought* to happen sometimes don't. The theory that moral temperament is first shaped (and misshaped) by craving the breast surely deserves a book of its own.

Most of us know from experience that children learn through imitation. It was not until fifteen years ago, however, that science began to understand exactly how this imitation happens and its effect on ethical learning. One summer day in 1995, neurologist Giacomo Rizzolatti was conducting an experiment on monkeys when something extraordinary took place. Rizzolatti and his team were studying the region of the monkey's brain involved in planning and carrying out movements. Each time the monkey took hold of an object, cells corresponding with that region in the brain would activate and cause the monitor to beep. Then came the eureka moment. A student of Rizzolatti's entered the lab holding an ice cream cone. When he lifted the ice cream to his mouth, the monitor started to beep, even though the monkey hadn't moved at all but was merely watching the student enjoy his afternoon gelato.

"It took us several years to believe what we were seeing," Dr. Rizzolatti later told the *New York Times*. In fact, the neurologist and his team had accidentally discovered a special class of cells called mirror neurons that had fired in the monkey's brain *simply because it had observed an action*. The human brain has mirror neurons that are far smarter, more flexible, and more highly evolved than those in monkeys, Rizzolatti later deduced, and with this revelation we entered a brave new world of moral understanding. Brain guru extraordinaire V. Ramachandran has suggested that the discovery of mirror neurons will provide a "unifying framework" for explaining everything from how empathy, language, and culture work to why some people are autistic. This discovery may well turn out to herald "the fifth revolution in human history," Ramachandran claims, "the 'neuroscience revolution' "—following the paradigm-shifting breakthroughs of Copernicus (the earth's not the center of the universe), Darwin (natural selection), Freud (the existence of the subconscious), and Crick (the discovery of DNA).

Mirror neurons are the brain's hardware for harmonizing individuals with their environment. The sole purpose of these neurons is to reflect *inside ourselves* actions we observe in others. "Mirror neurons allow us to grasp the minds of others *not* through conceptual reasoning but through direct simulation," Rizzolatti explains.

"By feeling, not by thinking." It is because of mirror neurons that you blush when you see someone else humiliated, flinch when someone else is struck, and can't resist the urge to laugh when seeing a group explode in giggles. (Indeed, people who test for "contagious yawning" tend to be more empathic.) Mirror neurons are the reason that emotions—both negative and positive—are so inexplicably contagious. They enable us to experience others as if from inside their own skin. In order to understand other people, we actually *become* them—a little bit—and bring the outside world inside by way of our own nervous systems.

Mirror neurons are the reason for the chameleon effect (the brain-to-brain imitation that causes babies to stick out their tongues when you do), as well as the Michelangelo effect, in which couples who've been married a long time begin to resemble one another by mirroring each other's expressions. As Daniel Goleman has pointed out, by mimicking what another person does or feels, mirror neurons create a shared sensibility, imprinting our neural pathways with imitated emotions. Seeing another's pain or disgust is almost exactly like being disgusted or in pain oneself. This maps the identical information from what we are seeing onto our own motor neurons, allowing us to participate in the other person's actions as if we ourselves were executing that action. Moreover, when we witness another being rejected, our brains "actually register the pain of social rejection," which is "mapped in the brain by the same mechanism that encodes physical real pain." Social emotions like guilt, shame, pride, embarrassment, disgust, and lust are learned in precisely the same way, from observing the responses of others, beginning with our parents.

As babies gaze out at the world, reading the faces and gestures of their caretakers, they are literally etching in their own brains a repertoire for emotion, behavior, and how the world works. A newborn baby, barely able to see, can imitate the facial expressions of adults within one hour of delivery. This motor imitation feeds the emotional system. Merely seeing a picture of a happy face elicits fleeting activity in the muscles that pull a child's mouth up into a smile. When a child unconsciously mimics the delight or sadness of a caretaker, this automatically creates a coupling between the baby's expressions and its emotions (this is also why physical behaviors such as smiling actually make us feel better—whether we're having a good day or not).

From the beginning, we respond to each other's feelings. When infants hear other babies crying, they howl, too—almost from birth—to show they are sympathetically upset. Mirror neurons appear to be linked to autism; some scientists believe that people with autism have "broken mirror" neurons that deprive them of bonding skills and empathy. (While many people with autism can identify an emotional expression, like sadness, or imitate sad looks with their own faces, they do not feel the emotional significance of the imitated emotion.) Mirror neurons also bolster the argument against exposing children to media violence. Neuroscientist Marco Iacoboni has cited increased "imitative violence in viewers" weaned on blood and gore.

Mother and Child

A COUPLE OF YEARS AGO, I was visiting an exhibit at the Cradle of Humankind, an hour's drive north from Johannesburg, South Africa, in the tiny village of Gauteng. This area is the site of the earliest discovered human remains, among them Mrs. Ples, the first adult *Australopithecus,* found here in 1947. In the steps-of-evolution exhibit, the model of *Australopithecus*—a four-foot replica in a glass case—bears more than a passing resemblance to the diminutive pop diva Chaka Khan, minus the hair extensions and leather culottes (the Neanderthal is actor Ralph Fiennes after a three-day drunk). The exhibit is humbling, to say the least, an upwardly mobile series of wax models fixed side by side in a graduated scale of humanness, from tiny simian creatures all the way up to strapping *Homo sapiens.* It makes you glad to be a human and upright, with Cuisinarts, blue jeans, and orthodonture.

Beside me in the line stood a stunning Indian woman wearing a gold and red sari. Her slender arms were adorned with dozens of bangles, and she was holding a baby no more than a few weeks old. The woman seemed to be as fascinated by the Stone Age figures as I was, and stood gazing into the small plastic eyes of an ancestor clad in an animal skin holding some sort of primordial hoe, while her infant daughter stared at her face. The baby's eyes were intently fixed upon her, absorbed by every flickering expression as she waited for the lovely woman's attention. I couldn't help watching this little dance. When the baby fussed, the mother looked into her eyes and the child settled down. When the woman smiled, the baby smiled. When she turned away, the infant scowled and screwed her eyes shut, kicking her feet and tugging the harness, as if the rays of the very sun had suddenly disappeared from her tiny world.

You learn the world from your mother's face. The mother's eyes, especially, are a child's refuge, the mirror where children confirm their existence. From the doting reflection of its mother's eyes, a baby draws its earliest, wordless lessons about connection, care, and love, and about how being ignored—which every child is sooner or later—makes the good feeling disappear. The mother's gaze (or the father's if he is the primary caretaker) determines more than you might realize about how you come to see yourself, your place in the world, and the moral nature of people around you. "The meeting eyes of love," George Eliot called this all-important connection in her novel *Middlemarch*. According to Dan Siegal, a psychologist who specializes in early parental bonding, every child yearns for—and must have—this eye contact for healthy emotional development to occur. Siegal, who founded a new field of research known as interpersonal neurobiology (IPNB), has proved that the mother's gaze plays a critical role in how we develop empathy. "Repeated tens of thousands of times in the child's life, these small moments of mutual rapport [serve to] transmit the best part of our humanity— our capacity for love—from one generation to the next," Siegal has discovered. Children deprived of the mother's gaze are likely to feel disconnected from others later in life. Many of them will struggle to heal this disconnect in destructive ways ranging from dysfunctional love to substance abuse. It was Carl Jung who described addiction as "a prayer gone awry"; indeed, there's an obvious link between the emptiness caused by a mother's absence and the spiritual impulse itself, with its goals of benediction, acceptance, and unity. Not long before his death, the late Pope John Paul II, who lost his own mother at an early age, was intrigued enough by IPNB—especially Dan Siegal's work on the mother's gaze—to invite Siegal to the Vatican for a private meeting to discuss how the pontiff's being orphaned had impacted his psychological and spiritual life.

Siegal suggests that the visual interaction between mother and child primes the moral organ in visceral ways. "Through mirroring, attachment to caregivers helps the immature brain use the mature functions of the parent's brain to organize its own processes," he told a journalist. "We *learn* to care, quite literally, by observing the caring behavior of our parents toward us." By the age of seven months, these earliest attachments have led to specific organizational changes in an infant's behavior and brain function. Having found a secure base in the world, according to psychologist John Bowlby, the founder of attachment theory, the child learns emotional resilience. If the caregiver is responsive to the child's signals and interacts with sensitivity, a secure attachment will be formed, reinforcing the child's own positive emotional states and teaching him or her to modulate negative states. Deprived of the mother's gaze, the area of the brain that coordinates social communication, empathic attunement, emotional regulation, and stimulus appraisal (the establishment of value and meaning) will be faulty. Such children are likely to develop "insecure attachment" along with all sorts of subsequent losses in self-esteem and feelings of not belonging. Infants whose mothers deliberately ignore them in laboratory experiments become agitated and distressed. Rather than crawl around like the babies being paid attention to, they stop exploring the environment and either brood alone or desperately solicit their mother for attention. Not surprisingly, children of mothers who display postpartum depression tend to be anxious and distressed themselves.

We've come a long way in understanding how harmful parental distance can be to children's emotional and moral development. Not long ago, popular wisdom held that in order for children to be self-reliant and well-behaved, parents should treat their kids as miniature adults. Before mirror neurons confirmed the vital link between empathy and parental attention, it was believed that children (little tabulae rasae) were best initiated right away into the sort of alienation they could expect as grown-ups. "There is a sensible way of treating children," behaviorist John Watson counseled in 1928. "Never hug and kiss them. Never let them sit in your lap. If you must, kiss them once on the forehead when they say goodnight and shake hands with them in the morning." How different this withholding approach is from that of the Kung people of the Kalahari, whose mothers deliver children alone without anesthetic, stay in almost constant physical contact with them for several months, hold them in a vertical position during most of their waking hours—the better to see them face to face—and nurse several times an hour for the first three or four years! Is it any surprise that the Kung are among the most peaceful tribes in Africa? Not only is touch "both the alpha and omega of affection," as philosopher William James famously wrote, it is connected to our body's production of the hormone oxytocin—also known as the molecule of love—which the vagus nerve instructs the brain to release during lovemaking, nursing, and other moments of connection.

Regardless of how they're raised, no other offspring in the animal kingdom come close to the intimacy shared by human parents and their young. Our unique evolution requires this close-knit bond. When humans finally, permanently, stood up on their hind legs, moving from tree life to flat savannah ground, *Homo sapiens* developed much narrower hips in order to walk upright. With the woman's pelvis narrowed for walking, human babies needed to be born prematurely in order to squeeze their already enormous heads through the narrower passage. Whereas other mammals are born only when their brains are more or less ready to control their bodies, human babies can do nothing for themselves. Once out of womb, these giant brains attached to helpless baby bodies need constant care, and this parental relationship—with its manipulations, give and take, and demands for justice, respect, and loyalty—becomes our ethical kindergarten.

In the complex relationship between parents and children, our earliest bonding patterns are formed. Our first glimmers of being loved by our mother, thereby knowing ourselves to be lovable, are indissolubly linked to our ability to care for others in our maturity. As anyone who's been a parent can attest, this love requires levels of patience, stamina, and selflessness beyond anything demanded by other relationships. Luckily, the rewards can be equally epic. Through the mirrored love in our parents' eyes, we learn surrender, devotion, and trust.

Venus and Mars

THOUGH WE STRIVE FOR GENDER EQUALITY in our politically correct, postfeminist world, our ethical lives are not immune to mammalian biology. We cannot understand men and women's different ethical lives without acknowledging these bodily differences. In fact, much of our scientific knowledge about empathy is drawn from studies on parenting and gender distinction, the odd ways that men and women differ in how we choose mates, remain faithful (or not), reconcile with each other in couples and groups (or not), and approach questions of selfishness, justice, harm, and respect.

Sex is an excellent starting point for understanding these differences. The anatomical difference between the sex cells of men and women is extreme. The human egg is eighty-five thousand times larger than the human sperm, and the implications of this vast disparity complicate human sexual life enormously. A woman produces only about four hundred eggs during her entire lifetime (of which only twenty or so can actually become infants). Men release in the neighborhood of a hundred million sperm with each ejaculation. As E. O. Wilson has described it, "Once he has achieved fertilization, [the male's] purely physical commitment has ended." Although the man's genes will benefit as much as the woman's his investment will be far less than hers unless she can convince him to stay and help raise the kids. That, of course, is the ethical rub.

"If a man were given total freedom to act, he could theoretically inseminate thousands of women in his lifetime, while women must protect their precious few children," Wilson writes. "It pays males to be aggressive, hasty, fickle, and undiscriminating . . . [and] for females to be coy, to hold back until they can identify the males with the best genes . . ." Female humans are relative prudes compared to our ape cousins, by the way; at their sexual prime, female chimps advertise their wares with a large pink patch of sexual skin, and for ten days during a thirty-six-day cycle, copulate several dozen times a day with every male they can get their hands on. Human males are "moderately polygynous," on the other hand, and initiate most of the changes in sexual partnership. While three-fourths of all human societies permit the taking of multiple wives (and most of them encourage the practice by law and custom), a woman's marriage to multiple husbands is sanctioned in fewer than 1 percent of societies.

Is it any wonder that marriage counselors, divorce lawyers, prostitutes, and the corporation that runs Hooters do such thriving business? Because women's bodies have seven times more oxytocin (the "love molecule") than men's, females commit more readily, and easily, than men do. While males tend to focus on autonomy, females emphasize relationship. Women need to be more selective about choosing partners, especially under short-term mating conditions, because they're the ones who must care for their young. Men get to have the commitment issues. Women, who need men to stick around, react more aversively to *emotional* jealousy, while men—who, before DNA testing appeared, could never be sure about a child's paternity (and inherit a primate aversion to supporting another man's offspring)—react worse to *sexual* infidelity. This isn't to say that women are okay with being cheated on—or that men are fine when they're emotionally displaced. But women do tend to focus on threats of abandonment while ape-headed, territorial males are fixated on the violation of their chosen female's nether parts. In the light of natural selection and biology, such common relationship issues start making greater sense. Women who have dependent children are more at risk from a mate who commits an emotional infidelity, while men are limited by the fact that they can never be certain of paternity because they do not bear offspring themselves. So another thousand Othellos are born.

The women's liberation movement was crucial to balancing the prevalent patriarchal way we used to think about moral issues. In 1975, feminist psychologist Carol Gilligan introduced the radical notion that care and kindness have as much to do with ethical wisdom as fairness and justice do. This feminine perspective was long overdue. Until Gilligan appeared on the scene, the party line had been that being good depended mostly on rules, laws, and the long arm of justice. This male-tilted emphasis focused more on autonomy than relationship, Gilligan argued—more on what was wrong with us than on what was right. The emphasis on rules and punishment implied that morality's first concern was to rein in human selfishness and brutality rather than to enhance love. Gilligan disagreed with this formulation. She suggested, instead, that empathy, connection, and care were the starting point of moral life, prefigured in the bond between mother and child and radiating out from there. This "ethic of care" emphasized relationships and interdependence over ethical impartiality. It focused on those individuals who are particularly vulnerable to our choices, giving extra moral consideration to need and unprotectedness. "Men do not know the women whom they say they love," Gilligan claimed in her landmark book *In a Dif-*

ferent Voice. "But while women have taken care of men, men have, in their theories of psychological development . . . tended to assume or devalue that care." Injecting emotional wisdom into a conversation dominated by rational principles and abstract standards, her theory personalized the way we think about human nature, with an emphasis on context, relationship, and the importance of being our brothers' keepers.

"Psychologists were studying white men and talking about humans," Carol Gilligan told me with a chuckle, when we met at an espresso bar in Greenwich Village. At seventy-two, Gilligan looks like she could be Carole King's long lost twin, with her Nefertiti nose and free-flying hair. "I always said that when women's voices entered what's called 'the human conversation' "—Gilligan makes air quotes and smiles—"that it would change the voice of that conversation. Thankfully, it has." In our therapy-laden, postfeminist age, it may be hard to appreciate how threatening Gilligan's juggernaut was at the time. The androcentric approach to morality had been that individuals have certain basic rights, which must be respected, and that in order for a society to work, restrictions must be imposed on what we can and cannot do. This is true as far as it goes, but it isn't the whole story. The feminist message that goodness is mirrored, cultivated, and honed by the imperative to care for others (the "responsibility" orientation) provided a humane balance to the predominant rules-driven "justice orientation." At first, there was great resistance to this estrogenic storming of the penile palace. Gilligan's male colleagues mocked her "touchy-feely" approach to ethics, the galling idea that feeling is as important as thinking. "The blind willingness to sacrifice people to truth has always been the danger of an ethics abstracted from life," she wrote in *In a Different Voice.*

Studies show that boys and girls differ in moral temperament from an early age. Where boys tend to be more focused on winning, girls are more interested in maintaining relationships even at a high cost to themselves. Frans de Waal, the primatologist, agrees with Gilligan that impersonal rights and wrongs are not a top priority for females; compromises that leave social connections intact are. When fights break out in groups of boys, the injured party is expected to get out of the way so that the competition can continue. When the same thing happens among a group of girls, the game stops while all the players gather around to help the girl who is crying. Is it any wonder that Mars and Venus collide in their opposing orbits of fair-versus-care? These different-not-unequal orientations can benefit from each other's example, however. While men are called on to grasp the possibility that there are no absolute moral truths, and that not all people have equal needs, women can be encouraged to separate feeling from thinking long enough to protect themselves from unfair treatment, and to curtail interactions that discount their independence.

Think about your own life. Are you aware of where your own stresses fall? How often do you sacrifice friendships on principle, for starters? Are you a person for whom winning is everything? How willing are you to negotiate for a win-win resolution to be achieved? Do you obey a monolithic belief in Truth—or will flexible, case-by-case truths suit you just as well? Would you rather be right or happy? Do you find yourself saying "It's nothing personal" a little too often? Or are you the type of person who takes things a bit too personally and lacks objectivity when you need it? Are you a follower when you should be leading, or someone who needs to be in charge even when you don't know what you're doing? Are you loyal to your group—whether it's a team, company, nation, or faith—even when they're in the wrong (as we find in the "don't snitch" policy popular among some gangs)? Or are you willing to speak truth to power even when it means standing alone, outside the in-group's popular ethic? Your answers to these questions will not correspond to black-and-white, male-female stereotypes, of course. We all know overly devoted, self-abnegating men and women who are philanderers. What's useful to understand is how these *orientations* affect your ability to make ethical choices. Neither approach is more right than the other, since both are needed for moral integration. "The heart is the seat of the mind," the Talmud tells us. One part without the other cannot make a whole.

Swedish researchers did an interesting experiment recently, showing how the mind can be tricked into being more empathic (a possible boon for both sexes). These scientists came up with a device that allows people to step outside their own skins and observe how their behavior appears to someone else. Using goggles linked to cameras trained on themselves, test subjects—in this case, a group of teenagers with anger issues—were invited to take a good hard look at their behavior from the outside in. Their brains tricked by optical and sensory information, these teenagers were able (through a sort of artificial mirror neuron system) to feel as if they were actually *in the body* of the therapist observing them. The results of such self-mirroring were remarkable. Researchers found that the human mind can "quickly adopt any other human form, no matter how different, as its own" through the creation of a sort of out-of-body experience. This empathy technology could turn out to be a watershed for marriage counselors attempting to help Mars and Venus connect; in fact, it might be extremely useful for anyone "more interested in changing everyone in their lives but themselves," the Swedes found. Think what this could do for the Mideast peace process. In a similar study using whites and blacks, researchers found that whites who spend time inhabiting black people's "avatars"—or virtual bodies—"become less anxious about racial differences." The scientists are calling this the Proteus Effect.

Perspective directly affects our feelings. These feelings then create our ethical lives, which arise from caring enough to notice how we behave with respect to others.

Emotions

TODAY, WE TAKE FOR GRANTED that feelings matter in human affairs—however complex, mercurial, perverse, or off-putting these feelings might be—but we forget that emotions were, until recently, the bête noire of the male-dominated sciences. "We all know that emotions are useless and bad for our peace of mind," B. F. Skinner declared in his novel *Walden Two*, echoing the feeling-phobic, male-dominated majority in the scientific community. Thankfully, baby, we've come a long way.

But what exactly are emotions and how do they dictate our moral behavior? Emotions are surges of affect or energy designed by natural selection to help us adapt to threats or other stimuli in our environment, philosopher Martha Nussbaum tells us. They are our intuitive guides to making our most important ethical judgments, honed by thousands of generations of trial and error to prepare us for life's possibilities. For an emotion to emerge, something has to trigger it, and though each emotion serves us in a specific way, there is no such thing as an emotional faculty. Each emotion more or less does its own thing, oblivious of the others, which explains a lot about why we can be so neurotic. Fear, loathing, guilt, anger, surprise, and contentment are all prompted by different neurological structures in the body designed to respond to corresponding stimuli. Look at guilt, for example, the iron maiden of emotions. We feel guilt when we harm someone in a social setting that is characterized by mutual concern. For instance, when people play repeated sessions of bargaining games, those who admit to feeling guilty are more likely to cooperate in future rounds. Thus, the emotion of guilt, so miserable to feel, serves a positive function as damage control, safeguarding us against cheating, lying, defecting, and breaking commitments (more on guilt in a moment).

By definition, emotions happen *to* us rather than being our choice. "Love is like a fever that comes and goes independent of will," Stendhal reminds us. It's not just love, but all our emotions, that operate beyond our conscious control. This is why proportion matters. That is why Plato used the allegory of a charioteer (the reasoning intellect) driving two horses, a white one (representing the moral impulse and the positive part of our passionate nature) and a black one (representing our concupiscent nature, including destructive passions and appetites). "Anybody can become angry," Aristotle counseled, famously. "That is easy; but to be angry with the right person, and to the right degree, and at the right time, and for the right purpose, and in the right way, that is not within everybody's power; that is not easy." We must measure our emotional responses to fit the specific details of the situation. Only then can virtue function.

What makes an emotion moral is the intensity with which it grips our mind, and the sense it leaves, "[different] from kindred non-moral emotions . . . [of] disinterestedness, apparent impartiality, and flavour of generality," as sociologist Edward Westermarck puts it. Thinking something is bad is different from thinking it's wrong, after all. Moral judgment suggests generality, the sense of how someone *ought* to be treated for no reason other than their being human. That is why emotions linked to personal preference and prejudice are too self-referential to be morally sound. (Wanting something does not make it right.) Moral emotions fall into four categories, according to Jonathan Haidt: "the other-condemning family (contempt, anger, and disgust), the self-conscious family (shame, embarrassment, and guilt), the other-suffering family (compassion), and the other-praising family (gratitude and elevation)." Without these involuntary commitment devices, we could not develop trust or form long-term, mutually beneficial relationships. While language can be manipulated, moral emotions can't. You can lie about how you're feeling, but you can't stop yourself from blushing when ashamed, or feeling disgusted by evil acts.

Emotions speak a language all their own. We've known this since the 1970s, when maverick scientists like Dr. Candace Pert redefined how emotions function throughout our physical structure. Pert, a researcher and pharmacologist, rocked the neuroscience world when she and a group of colleagues discovered the opiate receptor in the brain. A receptor is like a chemical lock on a cell into which a particular substance or key fits. A typical nerve cell has millions of receptors on its surface, each waiting for another molecule to wander by and bind to it. In the case of opiate receptors, this discovery showed that the brain is hardwired to respond to the body's internal mood enhancement system.

"It didn't matter if you were a lab rat, a first lady or a dope addict—everyone had the exact same mechanism in the brain for creating bliss," Pert told a reporter. Neuropeptides are "the body's biological correlate" to emotions, our most basic internal communication network. What this means is that emotion is the neurological language through which the mind and body communicate. What's more, these peptides are not limited to the brain, *we have emotions all over our bodies*—in our stomachs, glands, and major organs, anywhere that we find receptors. In other words, when you have a feeling in your gut, it's not just a figure of speech (since the stomach is thickly laced with peptide receptors). Anger and fear, sadness and joy, awe, pain and pleasure, are all over us—literally. Since emotions are regulated by neuropeptides, the brain's memory centers are filled with receptors for these peptides.

It is likely that emotion and memory are intertwined in ways we've barely begun to discover. That's why strong emotions are the key variable that makes us bother to remember things. Emotional memories are our earliest memories—long-term recollections stored for survival. Emotions travel in two directions, from brain into body and up the body into the brain. Pert uses a humorous example of body-to-brain emotion and how the mind puts a story on it. Let's say that a woman drops a cup of hot coffee in her lap. Her first reaction to the scalding is surprise and feeling pain. This sensation travels up her body till it gets to the level of the thalamus. That's when the woman thinks, "Oh, it's hotter than it usually is." "It's only when [the emotion] gets all the way up to the cortex that she can actually blame her husband," Pert likes to joke. "That's where we put the whole spin on it."

Nowhere is the body-to-brain interaction more complex and revelatory than in the realm of facial expression. In this field, Paul Ekman is the man. The world's foremost authority on the physiology of emotion, Ekman, who's seventy-seven and lives in northern California, nearly died three decades ago during a research trip to New Guinea. (He'd flown a Cessna into the jungle to photograph the faces of the indigenous people there and had been forced to make a nearly fatal crash landing.) Comparing the facial expressions of humans around the world, Ekman found that not a single emotion existed that could not be recognized by people everywhere. Next, he spent months of strenuous self-scrutiny with a hand mirror in an attempt to map the emotions on his own face—for which he was viciously mocked at the time by his peers—and created the FACS, or facial coding system, which, for the first time, explained how complex emotions are mirrored in the face. There are eighteen types of smile, for instance, from ultra-sincere to fake as a three-dollar bill. Compelling, too, was the evidence that facial expressions help to *create* emotion. When he grimaced, Ekman found that doing so elicited particular feelings (racing heart, anxiety). When he stuck out his tongue, as if disgusted, Ekman could feel his stomach turn over. We tend to think of emotion as a one-way street, beginning in our brain, but pioneers like Pert and Ekman have shown us that, in fact, our bodies are emotional superhighways with exits, entrances, overpasses, and merging lanes we never knew existed.

Ekman's research has helped us to understand how we make ethical choices. Using his FACS, he found that people with angry facial expressions tend to blame others for injustices. People with perpetually sad expressions, on the other hand, tend to attribute injustice to fate or impersonal factors. These "blame judgments" were proved to be guided by sensations arising in the viscera and facial musculature. And when it came to the smile, Ekman had a personal crash course in mirror neuron love. It happened during a week in Dharamsala, India, visiting the Dalai Lama. Ekman had traveled to the foothills of the Himalayas with a group of Western scientists to talk to the Tibetan leader in exile about the science of compassion. Ekman, who is not a Buddhist, claims to have felt something in the Dalai Lama's infectiously mirthful presence that he'd never encountered before in all his anthropological travels. "At the airport afterward, my wife looked at me and said, 'You're not the man I married!'" Ekman told me with a laugh. "I was acting like somebody who's in love."

Deconstructing such contagious benevolence, he detected four characteristics common to people with this transmissible power.

First was a "palpable goodness" that went far beyond some "warm and fuzzy aura" and seemed to arise from genuine integrity, Ekman explained. Next, an impression of selflessness—a lack of concern with status, fame, and ego—a "transparency between their personal and public lives that set them apart from those with charisma, who are often one thing on the outside, another when you look under the surface." Third, Ekman observed that this expansive, compassionate energy nurtured others. Finally, he was struck by the "amazing powers of attentiveness" displayed by individuals like the Dalai Lama, and the feeling one experienced of being "seen in the round," wholly acknowledged by someone with open eyes.

Daniel Goleman happened to be on that same trip but was already familiar with this uplifting phenomenon, which he'd first noticed among seasoned meditation practitioners in India while a Harvard postdoctoral fellow in the 1970s. These people seemed to exude what Goleman calls a "special quality, magnetic in a quiet sense." Contrary to stereotype, these spiritual types did not seem otherworldly at all. "They were lively and engaged, extremely present, involved in the moment, often funny, yet profoundly at peace— equanimous in disturbing situations," he told me. What's more, it seemed to him that this quality was communicable. "You always felt better than before you'd spent time with them, and this feeling lasted." One of the words used to describe this magnetic state is *sukkha*, a Pali term for "repleteness, contentment, delight—a calm, abiding joy regardless of external circumstances." *Sukkha* is selfless in nature and connected to a greater purpose—which is why it increases through service to others. Traditional cultures recognize that spending time with such elevating individuals is nourishing in itself. "People tune in to someone who is already in that magnificent internal space, catching it, so to speak, and carrying it to others," Goleman said.

Smiling has a lot to do with it. Anthropologists tell us that the human smile is among biology's greatest achievements. In our emotional toolbox of adaptations promoting cooperation, smiling is indispensable. Psychologists have called this the "happy face advantage"; we recognize happy faces more easily and readily, which is how nature fosters positive relationships among those who smile. Smiling is also good for your health. We know this from a famous long-term study that compared high school graduation photographs of a group of Mills College alumnae. It was found that those graduates with the warmest smiles reported less anxiety, fear, and sadness than their insincere sock hop sisters, and went on to happier lives. When smiles turn to laughter, cooperation levels soar. Laughter preceded language in human evolution, after all, and can help bond even the snarliest of enemies. In a deadlocked negotiation between Palestinians and Israelis in the 1970s, talks between historical enemies are said to have taken a "dramatic turn after they had laughed together," psychologist Dacher Keltner reports. In divorce studies, not laughing with our spouses has been shown to be more predictive of splitting up than not having sex.

Somatic markers are encoded in our gut feelings. Antonio Damasio, who first identified somatic markers, has found that they help us act smart even before we can think smart. Real-life situations require choosing between many complex and conflicting alternatives with a high degree of uncertainty and ambiguity. Cognition can go into overload, which is where somatic markers come in. Positive somatic markers operate by triggering good feelings in anticipation of good results; the negative markers work the same way. For example, giving money to a particularly adorable crusader for the homeless in my neighborhood—a cheerful woman whom no deluge of snow, sleet, rain, or gloom of night could stop from soliciting money for the poor ("A penny from your pocket! A dollar from your heart!")—always makes me feel good. Every day when I see her, a dollop of oxytocin leaks into my stingy heart. I anticipate the happy look on her face when I drop my few measly coins in her hand.

This is a positive somatic marker linked to the pleasure of helping. On the opposite corner to where she sits, a filthy belligerent drunk hangs out in his knit Rasta cap, hassling women with catcalls and muttering curses when I pass by without dropping a cent into his cup. Merely seeing him in the distance fills me with dread and loathing. This is a negative somatic marker linked to disgust. Both of these reflexive responses—which register first in the body, through sight (and in the latter case, smell)—have a different quality than reactions to nonmoral positive or negative stimuli (an ice cream cone or a pile of dog poop). Damasio explains that visceral markers are "installed" in us through repeated experience. Although these somatic responses cannot always be trusted (remember that emotion flares by way of association, not logic), they are "in the loop of reason," as Damasio puts it, as part of our choice-making process. Somatic markers provide the hunches (but not the conclusions) critical to deciding things. For patients like Phineas Gage with ventromedial prefrontal damage, there are no emotional hunches, and so they become social idiots. Without accurate feedback, we're lost in the world, unable to gauge or correct our behavior, deaf to our own inner signals. We can be seduced by immediate rewards that are likely to lead to harm and be put off by unpleasant immediate reactions—like parting with cash to help a stranger—whose rewards we should not doubt. We're tossed around by competing signals whose comparative values we cannot distinguish.

The ability to stand back from our impulses and make judgment calls stems from our higher cortical function, the uniquely human domain where things have names and names have stories and stories give meaning to our lives. Only we humans, in all creation, conceptualize ourselves in this way. Only we are conscious of the grounds on which we propose to act *as grounds*. We alone can stand back and see ourselves in the abstract; this is the meaning of self-awareness. An animal may be conscious of the object of its fear or desire, and experience it as fearful or desirable, and therefore as something to be avoided or sought. That is the ground of action. But a rational animal is also conscious that it fears or desires the object, and that it is inclined to act in a certain way as a result. This is what it means to be conscious of the ground as ground. We are able to experience not only rage, let's say, but awareness of our rage as well. That's why self-scrutiny is so important to emotional life. Once we're aware that we are being moved in a certain way, we gain a reflective distance from motive and story, and sometimes even make wiser choices.

The emotional mind believes what it sees, which is what makes it unreliable. We react to what we perceive and operate on the principle that what we perceive is reality. Since perception is subjective, our emotions are responding as if to a hologram projected through our own biases. While the reasoning mind makes logical connections between causes and effects, the emotional mind is indiscriminate, connecting things by flimsy association. "Entities can be like a hologram in the sense that a single part evokes the whole," in Goleman's words. That is exactly why our ability to have feelings about our feelings, and to appraise ourselves through the gimlet eye of what Adam Smith has called the impartial spectator, is so critical. Without such a "man within the breast," as Smith described our self-witnessing function, we can too easily believe our own emotional generalizations.

PATIENCE

The impartial spectator is what helps give us patience. Without patience, we cannot be moral. Without the ability to curb overweening reactions, forestall impulsivity, and delay gratification, we cannot exercise our ethical sense, which relies on a measure of selflessness and objectivity in order to function. In the book of Job, an allegory about how faith enables an ordinary man to withstand the coexistence of evil and God (or goodness), patience is the only antidote powerful enough to help one withstand the struggles of the conflicted world. The ability to hold our horses, prejudge probable outcomes, and choose behavior conducive to long-term goals saves us from our impulsive selves.

Ambrose Bierce, in the *Devil's Dictionary*, described patience as "a minor form of despair disguised as virtue," but we really would be wantons without it. Lacking an impartial spectator, wantons are helpless slaves of desire, driven by reptilian appetites with little or no ability to curb behavior in favor of predicted future outcomes. Though we take our capacity for patience for granted, it cinches our survival advantage over other animals. If you confront even the most patient animal with a temptation, it will wait for only a few seconds before being pulled in by the immediate reward. Compare this lack of self-control with the patience humans exercise every day in an array of challenges, and our advantage becomes clear.

Animals lack what's called "moral imagination," the ability to exercise patience for the greater good. "The imagination, by means of which alone I can anticipate future objects, or be interested in them, must carry me out of myself into the feelings of others by one and the same process by which I am thrown forward, as it were, into my future being, and interested in it," William Hazlitt wrote three centuries ago. Moral imagination is the brainchild of the neocortex, which governs inhibitory control and enables us to make projections about our own behavior and how others in our group are likely to treat us. Without the patience to perform the sometimes restricting tasks necessary for communal life, things like stopping for traffic lights, working monotonous jobs, and waiting for paychecks, our ultrasocial species could not survive. Patience is our primary means of escaping what sociologist Charles Tilly famously called "the tyranny of the here and now."

Our personal patience levels are established in childhood. Kids able to exercise patience have an unusually higher chance of successful lives later on, studies show. In tests where children are given the choice between taking a smaller reward (a marshmallow) immediately or waiting for a bigger payoff, toddlers who took the smaller reward were more likely to "end up as juvenile delinquents, alcoholics, gamblers, students with poor grades, and adults with unstable social and marital relationships," Marc Hauser tells us. Children who resisted temptation at age four were found, as adolescents, to be more socially competent, effective, self-assertive, and better able to cope with the frustrations of life. The ability to delay gratification and overcome stimulus control by only a few minutes had a radical effect on their ability to get into college and prosper.

We're (mostly) able to keep temptation at bay using a bag of physical and psychological tricks, prophylactics that fortify patience. This is called metathinking—outthinking ourselves—and even young children learn it. Such a thing as looking away from the marshmallow teaches kids how to distract themselves and delay gratification. Young children also use metaphors through which they transform delicious-looking marshmallows into tasteless clouds. Men play a similar game with women's breasts and mashed potatoes. Women may avoid shoe stores and chocolate shops to escape the lure of shopping or gaining weight. But our self-control is more powerful than even that. Our ability to inhibit immediate gratification also enables us to *change* life patterns. This is where neuroplasticity matters: *Changing habits changes our brains.* And changing our brains changes our habits. We're endowed with the ability to resculpt our brains through practice, beginning with the practice of patience. As anyone who's ever tried to meditate knows, this can be a hellish endeavor. The mind is an inferno sometimes, a leviathan at others, sometimes just a chatterbox, but always a worthy competitor in patience and attention. Meditators also know that the more you sit, the better it gets, because the brain learns to settle down. We nudge our plastic brains forward with each positive choice we make, even the bizarre one to sit on a cushion with our eyes shut.

We strengthen our patience muscle from infancy (remember the pissed-off nursing baby?). It's important to remember, however, that patience, like any moral emotion, has what Buddhism calls a "near-enemy"—a shadow behavior that comes when we take anything to an extreme. Two near-enemies of patience are lassitude and ennui, a paralysis toward change when it is called for (the near-enemy of righteousness is fanaticism; of generosity, becoming a doormat; of guilt, becoming guilt ridden; of frugality, stinginess; and so on). As we age, another near-enemy of patience—inertia—increasingly must be confronted. Like all social animals, our rules tend to acquire a fixed status. We tend to hang on to old habits, even if they backfire due to changes in the environment. As we age, this stuck-in-the-mudness only thickens. Stability and conservatism tend to take precedence over change, insight, innovation, and surprise. For this reason, most people become progressively less receptive to new activities and ideas as they grow older. They buy into the notion that age equals diminishment, the leopard has its spots, and they'd better stick with what they know. But people who continue to learn, experiment, and make mistakes as they age stay flexible in the middle ground between patience and change. They remain expansive, not constricted, and extend their imaginative horizons. An open mind promotes receptivity, creativity, and productivity in our daily lives.

Another near-enemy of patience, as crotchety middle-agers like me know, is stubbornness. Obviously, it's good to be stubborn in some situations—many an ingenue's innocence has been saved by fending off a drive-in date with a box of popcorn. Stubbornness can keep us recycling our trash when we hate to, patiently sorting metal and paper with our teeth clenched. But when character is bad, stubbornness can push it into despotism. Inflexibility is one of humanity's most fatal flaws. Adolf Hitler was famous for being utterly inflexible once he had made a decision. When someone suggested to the Führer, toward the end of the war, that some things might have been done differently, he became furious, saying, "But don't you see, I cannot change!"

GUILT AND SHAME

I learned about guilt from a maudlin B-movie my sisters used to watch and love. It was called *A Town Without Pity,* and its heroine was a German girl who was raped by four young American soldiers stationed in her alpine town. In the movie, the poor girl, whose only crime was her beauty, is mocked as a whore and treated like secondhand goods. During the trial, the lawyer for the defense, played by William Holden, is caught in the ethical nutcracker of having to defend these thugs, torn between destroying the innocent girl on the witness stand, and thus protecting the villainous soldiers, or doing what he knows is right. It was heartbreaking to watch the innocent victim turned guilty by the misogynist town mob.

A Town Without Pity was another ethical "blue coat" riddle for me, reminiscent of my first boyhood conundrum. It was easy to see both sides of the story; you could see how easily guilt and shame could be rearranged, exaggerated, or diminished by the perspective a person chose to adopt. The innocent girl could be made to look guilty; the GIs could be turned into victims of a Teutonic tart. This had resonance with my own family's drama as well. My mother was already a married man's mistress, everyone on our street knew that. We were objects of shame and judgment in our neighborhood. In spite of our bad reputation, though, I knew that we weren't bad people. A smart lawyer like William Holden could easily have mounted our case. But where was he when we needed him? I was baffled by the slippery nature of perceived justice. It seemed as if shame and guilt were movable pieces in the ethical jigsaw system. Shame was inflicted from the outside; guilt was a whip that one turned on oneself. Shame arises only when others become aware of a wrong we have done. When we feel guilt, it tends to remain private, arising as a feeling of remorse after a transgression, or when others believe that we're at fault. While guilty feelings can lead to atonement, fulfilling a positive moral purpose, shame leads only to defensiveness in anticipation of social rejection. Indeed, Carol Gilligan's husband, psychiatrist James Gilligan, believes that "the emotion of shame is the primary or ultimate cause of all violence."

Guilt implies a wrongful action, which requires amends; shame implies that a person is wrong in himself, and that nothing can be done about it. One feels guilty for stealing but shame for being a thief. We saw this after the AIG scandal, when public outcry over the exorbitant bonuses paid to executives of the bailed-out company led fifteen out of twenty bonus-takers to return the money, although it's unlikely the funds could have been retrieved otherwise. We feel shame for being bad people, guilt for doing bad things. A man may be ashamed of being poor or bald or flat-footed with the ladies. But he won't feel guilt unless he's Woody Allen, who could guilt himself over anything. We administer guilt when we feel that we've broken the rules—that's when the bad cop steps in and kicks our butt—with the degree of guilt being "proportional to the perceived importance of the social relationship with the victim," in the words of philosopher Richard Joyce.

Guilt operates on a system of internalized social rules. Having learned what causes disapproval in others, we tailor our behavior accordingly, conforming not only to the rules themselves but also to the beliefs behind them. This is why most of us feel guilty for social transgressions whether or not we're likely to be caught. Such conformity makes life easier for us. Instead of reinventing the moral wheel every time we make a decision, we're guided by an internalized compass whose chastening directions, including guilt, foster cooperative behavior. When social rules are fair and just, conformity is a good thing, of course. But when injustice and evil prevail, we may be forced to choose between obedience and integrity. Nature has installed "fail safes like blushing," as Frans de Waal reminds us, to ensure that guilt is more easily detected. This is why disobedience doesn't come easily to us. Our "uniquely human capacity to turn red in the face suggests that at some point in time our ancestors began to gain more from advertising trustworthiness than from fostering opportunism," de Waal explains. This warning system reinforces our sense of wrongdoing. Guilt deficiency is a sure sign of sociopathy. Not only do sociopaths not care what you think about what they're doing; they don't blush when they tell you so.

ANGER

Anger is a neutral, survival-based energy we can use for evil as well as for good. "Anger, with its poisoned root and honeyed tip," the Buddha called it, suggesting anger's ability to dupe us into moral aggression. Anger requires extreme attention to proportion, appropriateness, timing, and targeting. Later, you'll meet a double murderer named Tyrone Thompson who still feels no remorse for his honor crime, after thirty-eight years in prison. "I saw red," Thompson told me. "I knew what I had to do."

Just as righteous anger drives many to revenge, and prompts jihadists to murder for their faith, so may it activate moral behavior in others. Anger can be channeled toward the good. We're critical of aggressiveness, but without it mankind would have been dead in the water, literally. E. O. Wilson has identified no fewer than seven different kinds of human aggression, from protective anger to sexual anger to anger geared toward dominance, to the rage we feel toward predators and prey. Empathic anger, which sounds like an oxymoron but isn't, helps us to identify with others who've been wronged, and fight on their behalf. Since anger tends to be self-justifying, though, as well as morally blinding, it's too easy to cloak selfish anger in virtuous robes. Have you ever known a chronically angry person who claimed to be fighting for others but was actually a rage-aholic? Chronic anger is one of life's banes, wanton anger seeking its own release, ruining relationships, health, and morale. In one study, physicians who tested high for hostility in medical school were shown to be *seven times* as likely to have died by the age of fifty as were those with low hostility scores. Proneness to anger was a stronger predictor of dying young than smoking, high blood pressure, or high cholesterol. If you want to know where you fall on the hostility spectrum, take the hostility test at the end of the book. You may be as distressed by the results as I was.

Homo duplex struggles with the intensity of our moral emotions. The ferocious aggression within can overwhelm us. When Tyrone Thompson talks about seeing red, this is more than just a figure of speech. When rage grips the limbic brain, a scarlet veil of bloodshed from millennia past seems to color the rational mind. It's important to remember that we've inherited a "carnivorous psychology." Humans have lived 99 percent of their time on earth as hunters; we owe our biology, psychology, and many customs to the aggressive legacy of our arrow-toting, bludgeon-wielding, mastodon-felling forebears. In a very real sense, our intellect, interests, emotions, and basic social life all are products of this hunting heritage. For a long time, it's sobering to learn, war was viewed in much the same way as hunting (other human beings were simply the most dangerous game). During the past three centuries, a majority of the countries of Europe have been engaged in war approximately half the time. "War has been far too important in human history for it to be other than pleasurable for the males involved," one psychologist suggests. Like other outdated "pleasures," warfare as sport is no longer tenable in the modern world, clearly, where clubs and spears have morphed into A-bombs. But our carnivorous roots cannot be denied. It is easy to teach people to kill and hard to make them peaceable, psychology tells us, pointing to how easy it is to interest boys in fishing, fighting, and playing virtual war games on the computer. This innate aggression has bequeathed to us a lingering fascination with blood itself.

At a primal level of experience, blood is a very peculiar substance with moral implications all its own. One of three sacred substances that emanate from the body (the others are semen and milk), blood has long been equated with life and the life force. While milk expresses the female principle, and semen the male—and both have been considered sacred in many cults and rituals—blood transcends the difference between male and female as the universal substance. Though we're taught that bloodlust is wrong, blood's symbolic power as proof of sacrifice and self-transcendence is undeniable. Once, in a dusty town in Ladakh, India's uppermost province at the foothills of the Himalayas, a strangely lunar land that used to be part of Tibet and is filled with Buddhists and devout Muslims from the neighboring province of Kashmir, I was caught in a throng of Islamist believers—a crowd of a thousand-plus men—engaged in lashing themselves with knives and whips to commemorate the death of one of their martyred saints. Before I knew what was happening, I'd been sucked into this sacred riot (police on horseback finally fished me out), while all around me, ecstatic-faced men were cutting, gouging, and whipping themselves into a bloody frenzy and chanting together in Arabic. I had never witnessed anything like it: Their masochistic pleasure was almost contagious; they seemed transformed by the act of self-mutilation, liberated by their own bloodletting.

Ernest Hemingway found a different but related mystic release in the bullfighting ring, where the slow, premeditated, excruciating murder of an innocent animal is elevated to religious importance. One part of the mystery in the orgies of Bacchus involved eating the raw flesh of the animal together with the blood. At certain religious ceremonies it is the duty of the Hamatsa Indians of Northwest Canada to bite a piece of the arm, leg, or breast of a man. Some seven hundred thousand unfortunate souls were torn to bits by lions and other starved beasts to make Roman emperors popular at the Coliseum. This purgatorial bloodbath for the raging masses helped emperors of a death-obsessed culture keep the hounds of their populace at bay.

When we view our own unremitting aggressions in the primordial light of this hunting past, the intensity of our urges to attack, and to overpower, is easier to understand. We are, in addition to being compassionate, ferocious by birth, and contact with the life force of blood can be an intoxicating experience. "The human body bristles with power," wrote a reviewer of Elias Canetti's paean to human bloodthirst, *Crowds and Power*. "The most innocent seeming gesture recalls the primitive seizing and devouring of prey." If you've ever been to a crowded McDonald's at lunchtime, you know what this writer is talking about. We have a phylogenetically programmed, innate anger instinct that seeks for discharge and waits for the proper occasion to be expressed, psychology tells us. (There are opposing arguments on the hydraulic model of emotion release.) Zoologists suggest that if human aggression were more or less at the same level as that of other mammals—particularly that of our nearest relative, the chimpanzee—human society would be rather peaceful and nonviolent. E. O. Wilson disagrees with this view, insisting that studies of hyenas, lions, and langur monkeys, to name three ornery species, show that these animals engage in lethal fighting, infanticide, even cannibalism at a rate far above that found in human societies. "I suspect that if hamadryas baboons had nuclear weapons, they would destroy the world in a week," Wilson wrote in his book *On Human Nature*. "Alongside ants, which conduct assassinations, skirmishes and pitched battles as routine business, men are all but tranquilized pacifists." Still, most other animals are aggressive only in situations of crowding or limited resources, where people can behave cruelly and destructively in the most benign situations. Anger-prone people tend to eagerly await (and help to create) situations that permit their rage to explode.

This is why anger requires mindfulness. Repression, an underrated strength in a culture obsessed with liberty, is a faculty of mindfulness. Dedicated to the proposition that all men are created equal, and that all free men should let their freak flags fly, we underestimate the value of holding back, containing, suppressing, and sublimating in our cultivation of high-quality lives. More repression, not less, appears to lead people to greater happiness (in the same way that less choice, not more, seems to increase contentment). While this may sound reactionary to our freedom-obsessed ears, it's all about *what* we repress and how we repress it. Repression can be enlightening. Mindful self-censorship is more liberating than oppressive; ethics is a practice based on limits. Freedom and self-realization are not the result of blowing our top every time we feel like it. Rather, wisdom arises from knowing how violent our emotions can be and respecting that volatility, showing anger only when absolutely necessary. The Buddha, in his teachings on right speech, used three criteria for determining the wisdom of shooting off our mouth in any given situation. Considering what we have to say, we first ask ourself if it is *true*. Next, we ask ourself if it is *kind*. Finally, before we blast someone with anger, we must determine whether or not the assault is *necessary*. While we may not quite be able to hold ourselves to such strict verbal limits, they are handy to keep in mind. So-called repression can set us free.

The wonderful Vietnamese meditation master, poet, and peace activist Thich Nhat Hanh suggests that when we are feeling anger, we should try holding it in our arms with great tenderness. Bringing mindfulness to anger, the monk says, is like exposing a flower to sunlight. The flower cannot resist opening to the rays of the sun. When we're able to hold anger with love and compassion, Buddhists suggest, it can open to reveal its roots, which may spring from seeds of righteousness and mercy, covered over, distorted, turned red by aggression.

DISGUST

It's strange to learn that the emotion of disgust is the wellspring of moral behavior, and that disgust is a direct result of our carnivorous psychology. As meat eaters, we developed extra sensitivity to disgust as a way of not contaminating ourselves. In time, this literal aversion became symbolic disgust in our drive to transcend the dominion of nature, our emotional Jacob's ladder out of animality and toward the level of sacredness, where we hoped to disconnect from nature—almost.

Because humans love meat, disgust was shaped by natural selection as a guardian of the mouth, giving advantage to individuals who went beyond the sensory properties of a potentially edible object (this smells good!) and indiscriminate munching to thinking about where things had come from and what they had touched. Like rats, pigs, herring gulls, and cockroaches, we are omnivores. Disgust enabled our omnivorous species to forage through the world without poisoning ourselves. As a moral emotion, it does much the same. Disgust helps to protect our character from corruptive forces in the environment. Though we crave carnal experience, humans fear animality more than anything else, not least because, as animals, we are forced to die. Fearing mortality, we go to great lengths to hide evidence of our animal past, with disgust serving as the primary gatekeeper of our immortal human temple. Certain religions even sacramentalize love to exclude carnality. "The attempt to link love to God and then to cut away the sex is part of an elaborate defense against the gnawing fear of mortality," Haidt suggests.

An emotion that originates in putrefaction (and the universal gag reflex indicating expulsion of food from the mouth) comes to signify much more than microbe avoidance. Offensiveness and contamination are ascribed to people and things. Disgust takes on spiritual connotations; for the Hopi, the word for disgust is synonymous with "world out of balance." We feel disgust toward people and groups on the basis of skin color, sexuality, or whom they voted for in the last election. Disgust helps us navigate our way through the human zoo but also fosters prejudice (more on this when we come to stereotyping). One's subjective estimation of others ("I can't keep my hands off her!" "He makes me sick!") determines whether we view such individuals as good or bad. Our standards of disgust are entirely local, ridiculously local, and often abusive. A nineteen-year-old mother is stoned to death in front of her children after showing her legs in a Saudi backwater town while starlets cavort nearly naked on the cover of the *New York Post*.

Carnivorous psychology requires meat not only as food but also, weirdly, "meat" as a sort of moral opponent. Ethical disgust almost always involves some version of the bodily passions. Lust, gluttony, and greed are seen as debased, impure, and less than human. Those who live with the notion that the soul is in charge of the body—at least most of the time—cast stones at libertines for self-indulgence. We aspire to transcend our animal selves altogether and live as if we were demigods, spiritual visitors in a debased world subsisting on nothing but chastity and flesh-free entertainments.

But why does this food-related emotion extend itself so deeply into our social world? How do we go from rejecting a piece of rancid meat to stoning women to death for showing their thighs? Not only does disgust play a role in moral judgment, moral conflict, and ethnopolitical violence, it also has clinical links to obsessive-compulsive disorder and a variety of phobias. It's a short mental hop from the idea of washing away sins (rituals involving bodily purification or moral purification have been central to religious ceremonies for thousands of years) to the condition known as the Macbeth effect, induced when a threat to one's moral purity creates a neurotic need to cleanse oneself obsessively. The emotion of disgust develops runaway symbolic power, attaching itself to objects, people, and behavior considered to be immoral; disgust, escalated into rage, is certainly what gave us 9/11. Central to Al-Qaeda's loathing for Western infidel culture is disgust over our sexual mores. Many religions have extensive rules for regulating human bodily processes and keeping them separated from sacred objects and practices.

The trouble is that because disgust is a fast-action limbic response that bypasses reason, it can also be extremely reckless. Disgust is what fortifies walls of hatred, racism, and sexism. It plays a simple trick on the mind: Declare those you don't like to be vermin or parasites. Then it's easy to think of them as disgusting, deserving of exclusion, dismissal, even annihilation. The unconsciousness of our disgust responses makes them all the more dangerous—and sometimes ridiculous. Subjects in lab experiments are reluctant to wear articles of clothing that have been used by a stranger even if the article is well laundered. If the previous owner is believed to have an amputated leg or to have committed murder, their willingness to wear this clothing plummets further (we also don't like eating from dishes shaped like feces or drinking apple juice out of bedpans). Disgust says: once in contact, always in contact. Although this may be magical thinking, our queasiness cannot be reasoned away. We know how disgusting life could become without some call to purity, even when these aversions seem far-fetched. "The law only forbids men to do what their instincts incline them to do; what nature itself prohibits and punishes, it would be superfluous for the law to prohibit and punish," Westermarck reminds us sarcastically.

Wary of our doggish tendencies, the moral organ is primed to recognize animality in others—to recognize it with our bodies—just as we viscerally respond to goodness. "Hitherto unknown disgust, loathing, and fear" is what a friend of Dr. Jekyll's feels on first seeing Mr. Hyde, a creature subhuman enough to seem "troglodytic." We're physiologically prepared to smell a creep from across the room. We also feel disgust toward hypocrites. I was on a subway car the other day watching a lecherous old man eye a woman who appeared to be a prostitute with the hoity-toitiest look on his face you've ever seen, righteous contempt masking priapic fixation. His mock condescension was disgusting to me as I watched him ogle her fishnet stockings, then glance at the rest of us passengers to determine if he had been seen (and, if so, rolling his eyes judgmentally). Watching this moral charade on the train reminded me of how mixed up desire and fear are in us, how, so often, we secretly crave what we claim to despise. Look at Eliot Spitzer, the prostitution-flogging New York governor forced to resign after his own escapades with a hooker. Unexamined disgust can easily blind us to our own hypocrisy. Our lives become chronic fear reactions against what others tell us is wrong. We internalize moral presumptions that we'd do well to sort out for ourselves.

This purity reflex comes from the fear that, as animals, our lives will mean nothing. There's a poignant story about Cotton Mather, the Puritan pastor (and apologist for the Salem witch trials), recorded in his diary of 1654. While urinating against a tree, Mather happened to observe a dog peeing on another tree at the same time. Overwhelmed with disgust at the vileness of his own urination, mortified before his God, Mather shook his fist at heaven. "Yet I will be a more noble creature! And at the very time when my natural necessities debase me into the condition of the beast, my spirit shall (I say at that very time!) rise and soar." Amen.

ELEVATION

Just as we feel disgust when witnessing others (or ourselves) moving *down* the moral purity scale, so do we feel a corresponding, uplifting emotion when we find others behaving in virtuous ways. Haidt, who began his career researching disgust, calls this "elevation." Elevation is the penthouse floor of a building whose basement is seeped in disgust.

One of several self-transcending emotions—others are awe and admiration—elevation is among the more mysterious gifts of our mirror neuron system. The mere act of witnessing character, virtue, beauty, and truth tickles our vagus nerve, which stimulates oxytocin production and evokes in us, among other empathic behaviors, the desire to be better people living better lives. This is the power of someone like Barack Obama ("a vagal superstar," according to Dacher Keltner) to inspire multitudes to believe in a greater vision, *not* of him but of themselves. Elevation is not the same as happiness. As self-centered beings, we feel happy with our selfish victories and satisfactions. Elevation transcends that sensation and corresponds to moral beauty. Individuals with high vagus nerve activity (and more oxytocin) appear to be better at handling stress, building community, coping with bereavement, and breaking up conflict, Keltner has found. Elevation also differs from admiration for nonmoral excellence. When test subjects see awesome performances of death-defying feats—think of Philippe Petit, the lunatic Frenchman who tightrope walked between the towers of the World Trade Center—they report feeling chills and tingles, whereas elevation is a calmer feeling. We feel enlarged by displays of goodness, though elevation can annoy those resistant to it (as we saw among Obama detractors driven crazy by so much uplift). Heroism and aspiration make us aspire; witnessing courage can help make you brave; feeling hope in a world freighted with obstacles, despair, recession, and naysayers helps to make human life not only bearable but noble. We say to ourselves, if they can do it, why can't we? William James describes this beautifully:

> [The] new ardor which burns in his breast consumes in its glow the lower *noes* which formerly beset him, and keeps him immune against infection from the entire groveling portion of his nature. Magnanimities once impossible are now easy; paltry conventionalities and mean incentives once tyrannical hold no sway. The stone wall inside of him has fallen, the hardness in his heart has broken down . . . then [it is] as if our tears broke through an inveterate inner dam, and let all sorts of ancient peccancies and moral stagnancies drain away, leaving us now washed and soft of heart and open to every nobler leading.

There is a connection between the contagion of elevation and our idolatry toward unusually selfless people. Take Oprah Winfrey, who isn't selfless but is unusually big hearted (and encourages others to be the same way). To test the theory of elevation, Haidt and an assistant gathered forty-two lactating women together in his lab at the University of Virginia. Half of the nursing mothers watched a poignant episode of *Oprah* involving a rehabilitated gang member. The remaining group of nursing women spent their time watching an ordinary episode of *Seinfeld*. The elevation difference between these two groups was dramatic. The *Oprah*-watching moms overwhelmingly leaked milk into their pads (the sign of oxytocin lifting them up) and nursed their babies afterward. Hardly any of the *Seinfeld* watchers so much as wetted a pad. Elevation had made the *Oprah* mothers more generous and loving.

Elevation is not grandiosity. Vagal activity shifts our attention to *connection* rather than feeling superior to others—meaning strong enough to stand alone. When we behave reassuringly toward others in an I've-been-there-too-you're-not-alone kind of way, it's the vagus nerve doing the work. By inducing feelings of similarity between people, the vagus nerve calms down our fight-or-flight impulses. We have feelings of intimate connection spurred by the sight of other people's moral goodness. This is the elevation—and the outpouring of love—that believers seek in churches and temples (and secularists in nature and art). We needed to evolve such emotions to "turn off the I switch and turn on the We," as Haidt puts it. "Powerful moments of elevation seem to push a mental reset button, erasing negative feelings and replacing them with feelings of hope, love, and optimism, and a sense of moral elevation." The collective supersedes the self, at least while we're feeling uplifted.

Wonder and awe appear to serve a similar evolutionary function to elevation. The Greeks believed that Zeus gave human beings two qualities necessary for survival: a sense of justice and a taste for reverence (or awe). Goose bumps (piloerection) are the body's response to awe, apparently, a visceral response to the sense of self-expanding beyond our physical limits to merge with the larger collective. Awe is always prompted by contact with something greater than oneself. Two conditions must be met for awe to occur: First, we must perceive something vast (physically, conceptually, or spiritually vast, or oversized by fame); and, second, the vast thing cannot be accommodated to a person's existing mental structures. Religions have been our traditional method for promoting such peak experiences and for maximizing their ennobling powers. "By stopping people and making them receptive, awe creates an opening for change," Haidt reminds us. Atheist or believer, we all share the need for self-transcending emotions to counteract disgust.

There's a story I love about elevation. During World War II, the poet Anna Akhmatova read poetry over the radio waves of Leningrad—where food was so scarce that human flesh was being peddled in the streets—in a heroic attempt to help elevate her countrymen using the power of language and beauty. I picture Akhmatova in that radio station, struggling to remind the starving masses that sacredness still existed in the world. She read them poems about valor and love, and a light they had nearly forgotten, extinguished in them through suffering. Those who survived to remember this moment of courage, determination, and poetry spoke of it later in awestruck tones.

Emotional Intelligence

POETS KNOW THAT EMOTIONS are contagious. So do neuroscientists. Recently, I was sitting in a Tibetan restaurant in Northampton, Massachusetts, eating yak sausage with Daniel Goleman, the guy who helped redefine what smart means in our culture by moving from the old IQ-based model to one inclusive of social and emotional intelligence. Goleman is a onetime science writer for the *New York Times* as well as a thirty-year veteran of Buddhist meditation practice, which he first learned in India. Kindly eyed and kinky-haired, he talked to me passionately about scientific breakthroughs that have revolutionized our understanding of goodness and ethics, and how it is that "we're forming brain-to-brain bridges, all the time, with the people around us."

"We catch each other's emotions like a cold," he explains, digging into his exotic wiener. "The brain is programmed to be social." Of the four brain areas that are active even when we're doing nothing, he says, three are expressly devoted to dealing with relationships. "The brain's favorite show is relationships," he tells me. "That's because the people we love are our *biological allies.*"

"Biological allies?"

"Yes. If we're in a relationship with people who are constantly putting us down, or people in a distressed or toxic state, that has *biological* consequences. If we're around people who are nourishing, warm, and put us in a positive state, that has different biological consequences." In contact with loved ones, our bodies secrete oxytocin and endorphins, while chronically distressing relationships reverse that process, suppressing the immune system and raising stress hormones. "The importance of a particular relationship in your life will determine the power that each encounter with that person will have for you."

"What do you mean?"

"If your boss is in a bad mood," Goleman explains, "that can upset you in a way that no one else's mood can because you place more importance on what the boss does or says. You attune to them more, which makes their emotion pass to you more strongly."

Roles aren't the only determining factor in how others affect us: Sheer force of personality is another. Some people have more dominant emotional frequencies, both positive and negative, than others. We all know neurotic, miserable, self-absorbed people whose presence seems to suck all the air out of the room. Then there are the opposite types, those emotional super boosters who, like the Dalai Lama, infect those around them with positive feelings. "People go to these people just to hang out," Goleman says, chuckling. "Because they make you *feel* good. Imagine if we could all be like that for each other."

This is more than "kumbaya" for the brain science crowd, pie-in-the-sky pictures of happy folks swaying together in hormonal bliss. We are actually endowed with the power to direct, and perfect, the mood of a room or group of people with whom we are interacting. This power to shift a group's emotional tone is akin to what is called in biology a "zeitgeber" (literally, "time grabber"). Zeitgebers are things like the day-night cycle or music for a couple dancing, that switch our biological rhythms. When it comes to our personal encounters, the individual with the more forceful expressivity is typically the one whose emotions entrain the others. This helps to explain elevation, inspiration, and the power of charisma, as well as fanatically induced mob behavior.

That's why the company we keep is so crucial. "When we see someone else make a movement," Goleman reminds me, "our brain activates the centers for that movement. It's the same with emotions. The brain is designed to replicate inside us what we see other people experience. This is amazing. It coordinates everything we do with everyone else." In the absence of direct contact, our mirror neurons cannot generate empathy. "Our social brain was designed when social interaction was immediate," he continues. "In those days, early man knew about one hundred fifty people in his lifetime. Anyone there who was hurt, or in distress, he could help immediately. Now, we hear about people in distress on TV but are unable to actually do anything to help them—immediately. What can I do for a starving child in Ethiopia? The more abstract suffering is, the less it engages the social brain." Lack of engagement prevents compassion. "This is where the maxim 'use it or lose it' comes from in neuroscience," Goleman adds. "It means if we want to retain a skill such as compassion, we must *practice* it. That is what helps neurogenesis."

To illustrate this, Goleman tells me a story about his ninety-six-year-old mother. "She was a professor of sociology whose husband died many years before," he says. "She had a big house and decided to let an Asian graduate student [and his family] live there for free. Remember that Asians tend to value their elders. They see wisdom in them and *engage* with them. Well, this couple from Taiwan had a baby that lived to the age of two with my mother. This child regarded my mother as Grandma and treated her with great affection. During that time, I swear that cognitively, and physically, my mother seemed to get younger. It was stunning."

In the realm of social intelligence, no single distinction is more important than philosopher Martin Buber's differentiation between subjective and objective ways of treating others. In I-You relationships, we treat each other personally, eye to eye, whereas in I-It relationships, we treat the other person as a functionary, a means to an end. If you saw the film *The Devil Wears Prada*, you witnessed Meryl Streep being an imperious bitch goddess/fashion editrix treating the immediate world in the royal I-It. We all have both kinds of relationships. When you speak to a cashier are you talking to a person or a cash register? Do you care what this person has to say, if anything at all? Or do you treat their repartee as superfluous information, and would you mind just giving me my change, please? This distinction could not be more important. It's a lot harder to be an s.o.b. to a real-life person than it is to a machine with hands.

Social intelligence means moving toward I-You relationships. This switch can begin at home, with how we treat our families. Many of us have a tendency to treat our families as "family"— generic full stop—rather than, say, as themselves. We habituate to them and have the same conversations over and over, year after year, then wonder why these relationships become so stale. We can change this impersonal behavior by experimenting with the I-You approach, stepping from role-directed to individually directed behavior. If the family challenge is too much to face, and you would rather walk before you run (a friend likes to call family issues "Miracle-Gro for your character defects"), begin with a more neutral party whom you tend to objectify. Try shifting your perspective from "role" to "person" and see what happens. When I tried this myself, I noticed that the Korean sourpuss who runs my neighborhood deli, a grumpy-faced woman I never could stand, enjoyed humming church hymns to herself as she rang people up. One day, I bit the bullet and complimented her for having a lovely singing voice. This curmudgeon lit up like a hundred-watt bulb. Now, every time my deli lady sees me, she grins from ear to ear and tells me to have a nice day.

Virtual reality is not our friend when it comes to I-You relationships. In face-to-face interactions, one study showed, 55 percent of the emotional meaning of a message is expressed through facial, postural, and gestural means, 38 percent through the tone of voice, and only *7 percent* through words. In our twittering age of Facebook, text messages, and e-mail, the emotional implications of virtual blindness are legion. It's easier not to care (or to care much less) about names on a computer screen or profiles of disembodied entities changing their virtual monikers with a click of a mouse—than it is to not care about flesh and blood human beings. Virtual reality actually halts the feedback channel that our brain relies on as a way of anticipating other people's needs and the impact our actions will have on them. It's easier to fall into I-It nonsentiment and treat virtual entities as half human (or less). "The more *thems* we have," as Goleman reminds me, "the more dangerous the world becomes."

Free of face-to-face interaction, and the ability to mirror others, morality goes into cyber-freefall. "The story of evil in the world is so often a matter of hardware outperforming conscience," one journalist wrote. Nowhere is this more obvious than on the Web, where individuals are free to exercise virtual morality under pseudonymous cover with people they'll probably never meet. Our mirroring, zeitgeber-ing moral sense can't deal with a dimension free of tactile consequence. We pretend to be empathically linked to our chat buddy in Taipei, but the truth is that technology creates a false sense of intimacy (are your "friends" on Facebook really your friends?), rendering the immediate world both intimate and anonymous. The techno-creep of modern life fosters alienation, moral unease, and pseudo-relationships that would not exist without a Google search engine. We're challenged to redefine what connection even *means* in such an impersonal medium. Remember that the brain responds differently to impersonal versus personal stimuli. We deal with I-You and I-It relationships in different cerebral hemispheres. This is why, in virtual reality, where connection is both unnaturally easy and unnaturally fragile, we lose our way so easily. By deadening empathy, technology has the potential to disconnect us from feelings of real consequence. I recently saw a disillusioned Iraq vet describing this paradox on TV. Dispatched to the streets of Baghdad, he was surprised to realize how different real life in a war zone was from the video games he'd played as a teenager. This soldier, suffering from post-traumatic stress disorder (PTSD), had prepared himself for military violence on his computer, then been shocked to encounter the disconnect between virtual and real-life violence.

When Goleman and I leave the restaurant, the streets of Northampton are quiet. It's the middle of the afternoon. We walk together to my rental car without saying much. Then he shakes my hand and gives me his crinkly smile. We've been talking for two hours about what it means to be good; now I find myself staring at a parking ticket stuck on my windshield. "You can't win," I say, tearing it off. He pats me on the back and lopes away. In traffic, I find myself growing impatient; the old lady in front of me is driving too slowly; I need to get back to New York or I'll have to pay for another day's rental. Just as I'm about to slam the horn, I think about Goleman's elderly mother, and how happy that Taiwanese kid had made her. Empathy, the word, pops into my mind. The old lady turns a corner before I can blast her. "Empathy," Dan Goleman had said to me, "is the prime inhibitor to human cruelty."

Suckers, Grudgers, and Cheaters

Part Two

[JUSTICE/FAIRNESS]

If he does really think that there is no distinction
between virtue and vice, why Sir, when he leaves
our houses let us count our spoons.

—SAMUEL JOHNSON

We Tell Ourselves Stories

TWO PRIMARY INFLUENCES KICKED OFF cultural evolution in human beings. The first was the awareness of self and other, the transcendent ape-to-man moment when our neocortex became capable of empathy and we could walk in somebody else's shoes. The second was the appearance of formal language. Although Neanderthals grunted and cooed and hissed, it was not until around fifty thousand years ago that humans gained full linguistic ability. This ability to put our feelings into words, and use our words to build a life together, began the snowballing cultural effect that E. O. Wilson calls "hypertrophy." Once we had languages with which to engage in discussions and tell stories, moral practices could be put into place.

Why does ethical conduct require language? Because self-control requires language. Our behavior is determined by what we tell ourselves is right and wrong. Also, what we call the "self" (another uniquely human concept) would not exist were it not for language. The self-image we form is largely based on the stories we tell ourselves *about* ourselves (based on experience, memory, and personal belief). But how we conceptualize ourselves is not how we really are. We go through our lives, every one of us, with a degree of "self dysmorphia" (just as anorexics suffer from body dysmorphia), a distorted image of our own character. Language is indispensable to how this self-shape comes into being within our own minds. When we listen to our minds in the process of confabulating reality, using semantics to strengthen one argument over another as we appraise a given situation, and our ethical position in its regard, this becomes obvious.

In order to think about ourselves, we must create a narrative. For purposes of self-determination, each of us *is* his or her story, in fact. The self we believe in gives us an inner world full of simulations, social comparisons, and reputation concerns. This self also comes with an inner sadist, a contrarian voice that seems to enjoy tormenting us, to test our mettle, to challenge our motives. It is because of this self that we're able to make distinctions between right and wrong in the first place. Without the ability to sort mental impressions into words, we might have bits and pieces of thought derived from images, but in order to plan things, weigh pros and cons, and analyze past success and failure, we must have formal language. We know what we think when we find the right words. The writer Joan Didion, who famously wrote in her book *The White Album* that "we tell ourselves stories in order to live," admitted to me that until she actually writes something down, "I don't even know what I *think*!" Without language, ethics itself is kaput.

To create systems of fairness, justice, loyalty, and so on, early humans set about experimenting with various sets of "normative resources"—rules, stories, myths, images, and more—to define, and refine, the way in which we ought to live. "Ought" is the operative word here: The leap from *is* to *ought* was our first step toward becoming moral beings, extrapolating general codes of conduct from successful social strategies for individual and group integrity.

Animals may arrive at a nonverbal consensus about what kinds of behavior to tolerate, or forbid, in their midst, but without language, the principles behind such decisions could not be conceptualized, let alone debated. To communicate intentions and feelings is one thing; to clarify what's right and what's wrong—and *why*—is another.

It's funny to learn that ethics would never have evolved without gossip. In the beginning, anthropologists tell us, "language evolved as a replacement for physical grooming." Our human shift from picking each other's lice to minding each other's business appears to have been a natural progression for our nosy species. Gossip has been an indispensable method for policing one another ever since, helping us to monitor good and evil as well as prevent physical conflict. In fact, gossip is our first line of defense before violence in the exertion of social control, Haidt suggests. Before we punch someone in the face, or torch his house, we can always ruin his reputation. A good reputation is social collateral, and gossip is key to how we protect it. As a moral controlling device, it allows us to save face and cast aspersions on others. We are not autonomously moral beings, after all. The more closely people live together, the more they care; the more they care, the more they gossip; and the more they gossip, the more language can serve its ethical function. "Gossip paired with reciprocity allows karma to work here on earth, not in the next life," a psychologist quipped.

We care deeply about how others see us. Unfortunately, our private self and the one we present to the world may be at odds with one another, as we saw with the lecher and the prostitute on the subway car. It's entirely possible to put up a good front and be a dirty rotten scoundrel underneath. "The image of myself which I try to create in my own mind in order that I may love myself is very different from the image which I try to create in the minds of others in order that they may love me," the poet W. H. Auden confessed in his essay, "Hic et Ille." As social chameleons, most of us are willing to fake our colors—at least some of the time—to gain approval and avoid rejection. How much we're willing to dissemble, or even lie, when the majority are pulling in a direction we don't agree with determines how morally sound we are. In obvious and subtle ways, our characters are tested every day in this tension between conformism and conscience.

People in all societies gossip, and the first rule of life in a dense web of gossip is: Be careful what you do. Humans use language primarily to talk *about* other people, to find out who's doing what, who's sleeping with so and so's husband, who cheated whom, who behaved heroically or who caved in. Indeed, gossip tends to be overwhelmingly critical, concerned primarily with moral and social violations. This is because individuals who were able to share information had an advantage in human evolution. Our ancestors surmised that, in a gossipy world, what we do matters less than what people think we do, so we'd better be able to frame our actions in a positive light. As ultra-social creatures, we're also ultra-manipulators, fabricators, and competitors for the driver's seat; gossip created "a runaway competition in who could be master of the art of social manipulation, relationship aggression and reputation management" in human society, as E. O. Wilson tells us. We also learned to prepare ourselves for other people's attempts to deceive, compete against, and manipulate *us*.

As a species, we love to gab. From metropolitan centers to the primitive ends of the earth, we are language drunk, addicted to stories. An observer of the Kung bushmen verified this garrulous tendency toward universal comeuppance. "There is an endless flow of talk," he observed,

> about gathering, hunting, the weather, food distribution,
> gift giving, and scandal. No !Kung is ever at a loss for words,

and often two or three people will hold forth at once in a single conversation, giving the listeners a choice of channels to tune in on. A good proportion of this talk in even the happiest of camps verges on argument. People argue about improper food division, about breaches of etiquette, and about failure to reciprocate hospitality and gift giving . . . Almost all the arguments are *ad hominem*. The most frequent accusations heard are of pride, arrogance, laziness, and selfishness.

Gossip and storytelling allow us to pool the wisdom of communal emotion. Our chatter eventually amalgamates into systems of ethical conduct. Moral emotions like gratitude, contempt, and anger can be verbalized to create the *shared* sense of right and wrong that allows us to live together. Reciprocity is central to how gossip works. Have you ever noticed how hard it is *not* to share dishy information? (A friend of mine calls this "emptying the ashtrays," referring to the irresistible gossip between friends following a party.) That's because our brains are wired to pay stories forward. Once you've unburdened yourself ("I just can't hold this in!"), it's likely that others will reciprocate in kind, divulging some tidbit of their own. We may judge indiscretions as a moral liability ("loose lips sink ships"), but indiscreet sharing is also a form of social insurance, as well as a source of intimacy. As a memoir writer, I've received hundreds of intimate letters from readers who felt compelled to divulge (sometimes shockingly, once criminally) personal things to me simply because I'd been honest with them in a book. These letters ranged from poignant to obscene, but the content isn't the point. It's the automaticity of the gossip reflex that matters, and the reason behind this is central to the cost-benefit side of morality. Communication is a non-zero-sum game where both players stand to win. It costs us nothing to share information and both parties are likely to come out ahead. We're able to sharpen our ethical nails on gossip and scandal, and to feel contempt, a central moral emotion, as well as superiority, while being asked for nothing in return. Character assassination can also be morally damaging to the gossiper and turn all of us into hypocrites, of course. "In our condemnation of others' hypocrisy we only compound our own," Haidt warns. Hypocrisy is a tribute vice pays to virtue, after all.

Clever individuals manipulate language (as Bill Clinton did when questioning what the definition of "is" is during the Monica Lewinsky scandal) and use semantics to obfuscate the truth. Hypocrisy thrives in our language-driven culture; sociopathy, too. A landmark study of prisoners showed that psychopaths process emotional words like "hate" and "love" differently from the way normal people do, using inappropriate parts of their brains. Instead of showing activity in the limbic system and midbrain, where emotions are meant to be processed, psychopaths showed activity only in the language center at the front of the brain. This makes them capable of understanding emotions only linguistically, "as if knowing the words but not the music."

We "hear" right and wrong in the same way we pick out harmonious or discordant notes in music. The moral sense depends on such hearing, which in turn depends on our prejudices. If this sounds complex, that's because it is. Since the moral sense is as prone to illusions as our other senses, the sound of right and wrong can be used to clarify or to cover up the truth. We "understand" moral issues similarly to how we "understand" the acoustic grammar of Beethoven or Joni Mitchell, using built-in cognitive grooves receptive to these stimuli. Though these sensors can be duped, they are accurate much of the time. The immune system could have responses to a massive number of molecules, but due to early experience it ends up locking onto only a few; the linguistic system could build a massive number of expressed languages, but due to experience with the native tongue, it focuses on specific parameters in order to master the first language; and the moral system could respond to any number of stimuli, but fixes on the ones that most directly affect our lives, choosing our battles in a world filled with competing interests.

Morality is unconscious in the way that language acquisition is. If you had to think of noun, adjective, and so on every time you started talking, you wouldn't be able to communicate. Similarly, psychologist Marc Hauser assures us, "If every time you were confronted with a moral issue, you had to work it through, you would do nothing else." That's why stories, especially parables and fiction, are so integral to passing wisdom along. They're heuristic devices, shortcuts, to insight, communicating universal truths about our behavior and the lessons we might draw from more carefully observing it. For at least the past forty thousand years, our species has used stories to teach itself about good and evil and enable us to consider alternative versions of what is around us. Our ethical repertoires are widened by imagination. Although Victor Hugo lived two centuries ago, the question of what we'd do in Jean Valjean's place (go to prison for stealing a loaf of bread to feed our hungry family, or obey the law and watch them starve?) still arrests our moral imagination.

The received wisdom of stories allows us to create a sense of self. Character is composed of three levels, psychologists tell us: basic traits, characteristic adaptations, and life story. On a foundation of genetic inheritance and cultural influence, "our minds construct an evolving story that integrates a reconstructed past, perceived present, and anticipated future into a coherent and vitalizing life myth," writes Richard Tedeschi. Each of our "life myths" is, in fact, a work of historical fiction. Like all fiction, the stories we tell ourselves—about ourselves and what we're made of—are different from reality.

Who Am I?

THE LIFE MYTH IS COMPOSED by labeling experience as "good" or "bad." These labels dictate how experience is imprinted in our minds as reality. This is useful to remember when considering our own changing perceptions of things, especially outdated and primitive responses. Though we can't help labeling things, there's a built-in flaw to the system of automatically marking things we don't like as bad and those that please us as naturally good. Philosophers have recognized this for ages. "When people see some things as beautiful, other things become ugly. When people see some things as good, other things become bad," Chinese philosopher Lao Tse warned. We spend our lives bifurcating situations into opposing camps of what we approve of, or desire, and what we don't, and then tell ourselves that this is reality.

The mistake of this is obvious: Our knee-jerk opinions, tastes, and proclivities are not the truth, and feelings aren't facts, especially since we're biased. The moral sense, though hardwired, is not always right. Just because a particular word, thought, or story resonates negatively or positively in your psyche doesn't mean you're not deluding yourself. There are eternal truths and temporal truths, universal moral tenets and localized cultural bigotries. Unless we understand the automaticity of the labeling response and how unthinkingly we absorb social ideas (which may have nothing to do with right and wrong), we can't begin to think for ourselves.

Opinions are like fashion, fads, and weather—they rotate with the changing seasons. Morality is another thing. Remember what Lillian Hellman, the left-leaning playwright, told the House Un-American Activities Committee? "I do not cut my conscience to match the fashion of the time." In the flip-flopping of lovers' hearts, in our shifting interpretations of fairness—entirely dependent on social conditions—and in loyalties rearranged by betrayal, expedience, and information disclosure, we discover our own moral organ shaken and stirred. That is why it's advisable to question *why* certain things trigger strong feelings of like and dislike in us; and how much of our emotional response is inherited, and prejudicial, and how much true, fresh, and personal. To what degree are your responses to different issues a result of the story you've told yourself, the labels you've pinned on such and such an experience (this is wonderful, that was awful)? And how long after evidence to the contrary has appeared might you still be clinging to the wreckage?

Belief is inseparable from memory, and memory is inseparable from our sense of self. Without memory, we could not remember ourselves. Without language to articulate our life myth daily (notice how many times a day you reflect on being the kind of person who does or doesn't do this or that), we would literally forget who we are. Without proper left-brain functioning, we actually lose track of ourselves. In a sense, we melt into everything else and life becomes oceanic. This is exactly what happened to Jill Bolte Taylor, a Harvard-trained neuroanatomist who suffered a potentially fatal brain bleed in 1996. The stroke incapacitated her left brain, the boundary-making, reason-abiding, language-producing hemisphere—and caused a personality meltdown that changed Bolte Taylor's "self" image forever.

Alone in her Cambridge, Massachusetts, apartment, the thirty-five-year-old researcher awoke on the morning of December 10 with a piercing pain directly behind her left eye. As the pain grew, subsided, and increased again, it brought with it a powerful sense of dissociation that seemed to roll over her. Bolte Taylor was strangely detached from normal reality, though lucid, as if watching herself from outside her own body, or in "the playback of a memory," as she told me when we spoke. In *My Stroke of Insight,* her memoir about this transformative, frightening episode, Bolte Taylor writes, "As the language centers of my left hemisphere grew increasingly silent and I became detached from the memories of my life, I was comforted by an expanding sense of grace"—although she was actually wedged in a bathtub, helpless, unable to move. Then this hard-headed scientist proceeded to have an experience any mystic would write home about:

> Wow, what a strange and amazing thing I am. What a
> bizarre, living being I am. Life! I am life! I am a sea of water
> bound inside this membranous pouch. Here, in this form,
> I am a conscious mind and this body is the vehicle through
> which I am ALIVE! I am trillions of cells sharing a common
> mind. I am here, now, thriving as life. Wow! What an
> unfathomable concept! I am cellular life, no—I am molecular
> life with manual dexterity and a cognitive mind!

If there's such a thing as nirvana envy, this could turn you green. "It was the most beautiful experience you can imagine," Bolte Taylor told me. "I felt eternally, unconditionally connected to everything around me. This has permanently changed how I feel, and how I relate to other people."

"How?"

"I'm not at the 'effect' of my thoughts so much now," she said. "I now know what it's like to be free of this oppressive voice of the self that's constantly bossing you around."

"But we need a self to remember what's right and wrong," I suggested. "Otherwise, what happens to self-control?"

"We learn to recognize the other hemisphere of our brains," Bolte Taylor insisted. "As a society, we do not focus on what someone has *gained* in the absence of something they have lost. 'Good' and 'bad' are just left-brained labels. The right brain doesn't label things."

As a dominantly left-brained culture that prizes control, success, progress, status, and particularity of mind and thought as the best way of being, we downplay right-brain surrender, flow, release, and ineffability for being not quite "grown-up." They sound airy-fairy, passive, and noncommittal, and we really don't want any part of them. This left-brain imbalance in a male-dominated world is what helps to make us aggressive, stressed, overextended, and all hung up on meaningless details multiplied by techno-creep. We're all about pushing, most of the time—pushing ourselves to live our best lives, dammit, or fall off the cultural escalator. It's enough to make you crazy sometimes, this Babel of achievement in your brain, this pushing, punishing side of the mind that wants to conquer every moment. It's the opposite of the kind of awareness that Bolte Taylor found in that bathtub. "Our left brain is all about push," she told me. "But the right brain is about *pause*. You have to have both, the push and pause, right and left, for balance. We're designed for both. I can now identify clearly when I am in the push or pause."

"Really?"

"I can feel it in my body," she said. Right-brain awareness, as Bolte Taylor describes it, sounds like a chat with Candace Pert's opiate receptors, organ to organ, bypassing the rational mind. "I prefer the pause because it feels better," she explained. "It's more joyful and cooperative. People like me better. At the same time, I can use the tools of the left hemisphere to push into the world. But as soon as it becomes stressful, I can feel that in my body. I'm able to avoid the negative effect, the wear and tear on my body. I believe it's a skill we can develop."

We underestimate the power of our bodies, and the power of thought upon the body, when considering how our life stories grow. This sounds abstract but it's not. Remember that communication happens nonverbally, by and large. Our nonverbal apparatus is far more refined than we know. People with damage in their left hemisphere often cannot create or understand speech, but may be geniuses at knowing if people are lying. (Those with right-brain damage often cannot appropriately assess emotional content.) While our left brain listens carefully to words, interpreting, weighing, and discriminating, our right brain interprets nonverbal communication, subtle cues like tone of voice, facial expression, and body language.

Just as the receptors in our tongues guide us to good foods and away from bad foods, our right brain (predominantly) guides us toward some people and away from others, depending on intuitive clues. In survival situations, our gut reactions are nearly always more trustworthy than cogitation, the story we tell ourselves *about* what's happening. The trouble is that our moral organ, so intimately wired to the limbic system, errs on the side of negativity, prejudice, stereotyping, and phobic responses geared to the Ice Age. This is hard to understand. Our instincts are both our best resource *and* our worst saboteur. Ancient man, in his dangerous world, needed lots of negativity to protect himself from outsiders and saber-toothed tigers. It was better to be safe than sorry when it came to the survival response. This means that we've inherited ethical wiring both obsolete and indispensable. This is our challenge and our scourge, parting the reptilian from the humane.

Composing our life myth is a process that starts in childhood.

Studies show a paradoxical relationship between one's sense of self and how our parents describe their own childhood, their family, and their own coming of age. Our first narrative mirroring comes from reflecting our parents' life story *as they tell it*. Using an instrument called the Adult Attachment Interview, psychologist Mary Main invited a group of parents and children to participate in a study on language and bonding. She asked the parents to tell the story of their own childhood and found that *how* parents told their story, how they established their identity in the mind of their child, was the most powerful predictor (85 percent accuracy) of whether their children would be securely attached to them. How we attach to our parents has a lot to do with how we behave in the world later on. If adults could create a "reflective, coherent, and emotionally rich narrative about their own childhoods," the psychologist found, "they were likely to form a good, secure relationship with their children— no matter how 'insecurely attached' they themselves had been as children or how inadequate or even abusive their own parents were."

It wasn't what happened to them as children, but how they came to make sense of what happened to them, that predicted their emotional integration as adults and what kind of parents they'd be. It also predicted what sort of self-concept they would pass along to their kids. The story was the vehicle.

"Ought" Does Not Exist in Nature

JUST AS WE COMPOSE A LIFE MYTH by labeling our experiences, so do groups operate on the principle of "consensus reality." Consensus reality is the agreed-to truth of any given social group—what we believe to be good, bad, right, wrong, moral, immoral, or just plain disgusting. A group of revelers at Mardi Gras have a different consensus reality than members of a religious cult where women wear gingham down to the ankles, sporting hairdos from *Little House on the Prairie.*

Having mirrored the outside world inward as children, and formed ourselves from behavior and beliefs swirling around us in the environment, we're raised to accept our own group's customs and reject those of other groups. We agree to live *as if* our rules, laws, and dictates are worth obeying, while the moral undergirding of those rules changes simply by crossing a geographical border. In India, it's appropriate to kill young brides whose husbands die or no longer want them. The males who perform these crimes are respectable members of their community for having done the "right" thing. We ask ourselves how this can be and feel righteous in our indignation. Our opinion may even be correct (how can burning women not be wrong?), but the fact remains that someone, somewhere, will find any given behavior acceptable, and the wheel of suffering will keep on spinning. This is because truth is different from Truth and consensus reality is not the Truth. The Truth exists beyond us-here-now or it cannot be classified as moral. Customs are different from ethical wisdom. Also, "ought" does not exist in nature. "Ought" is the creation of our precious left brain, the storytelling hemisphere, which dictates our personal value system. "It is difficult to get a man to understand something when his salary depends upon his not understanding it," Upton Sinclair deadpanned. Survival justifies ethical blind spots.

We mistakenly squeeze "ought" from "is." Philosophers call this the naturalistic fallacy. Most of us do this every day of our lives without realizing it. We obey the "oughts" of our consensus reality and call them gospel. Women are physically weaker in the animal kingdom, which must mean, for instance, that they are to be dominated. Just look at the wildebeests. When we claim that because something exists in nature, that makes it right, or that when things do not appear in nature, that makes them wrong, we really have drunk the Kool-Aid. Like cult members agreeing to a mass hallucination, we've consented to pretend that wrong is right. The naturalistic fallacy can lead us to lynching (integration isn't "natural"), to infanticide (male grizzly bears kill their young), and to throwing virgins into the bowels of volcanos (after ripping their hearts out while they are still alive) because the mountain God is hungry for pubescent female flesh and must be appeased to avoid an eruption.

We believe our *ought* to be what *is*. But how does the brain conjure "ought" from "is"? "To dislike something is very different from disapproving of it," as philosopher Richard Joyce notes. The answer to this riddle lies in a psychological process known as projectivism. Projectivism in philosophy involves the attribution of qualities to an object *as if those qualities actually belong to it*. The Scottish philosopher David Hume put it like this in *A Treatise of Human Nature*: " 'Tis a common observation, that the mind has a great propensity to spread itself on external objects, and to conjoin with them any internal impressions, which they occasion. [Just as] beauty is not a quality of the object, but a certain feeling of the spectator, so virtue and vice are not qualities in the persons to whom language ascribes them, but feelings of the spectator." From the privacy of our own minds, we simulate the world, coloring it with our likes and dislikes, then break into the privacy of other minds (what would so-and-so think?) with our own beliefs and opinions.

We believe in the truth of our own projections—some of which originate with personal bias, most of which arise from genetic and cultural predispositions—and live as if our responses were based in fact. We are motivated by our ideas about things, not the things themselves, which in turn depend on the story we believe in. Everybody knows that the same situation through different eyes turns into different movies. Let's use Hume's famous example of a suffering animal found in a forest. You come upon the animal and see it as deserving—indeed, requiring—your pity. Stricken with emotion, you don't understand that "this quality of pitifulness," as Hume calls it, "is the new creation your own mind has conjured." Someone else might not have given the creature a second thought. Holding the wounded animal's head in your hand, you believe that the pitiful nature of the event is the "parent of the sentiment" but it is, in fact, "emotion's child." The emotion comes first (poor little kitty!) followed by the thought, "I am morally obligated to relieve its suffering."

The "ought" is a mental fabrication, cold as that sounds to our kitty-loving ears. According to Richard Joyce, there is "no evidence that the human moral sensibility functions anything like a perceptual organ, detecting moral properties in the world." Knowing how projectivism works can help us see through our own melodramas and bigotries. Because projectivism is so willy-nilly, we need laws, punishment, and a modicum of ethical consensus in order to cooperate. But there is hypocrisy hidden in "ought." The loop between perception, feeling, and judgment is so infinitesimally quick that we're unaware of painting the world with a palette of moral opinions mixed inside our own brains.

The question is: How can we know what's real and what isn't? If no objective standard for right and wrong exists, what is to stop us from winging it? The answer is nothing—which is where free (or free-ish) will comes in. Helped by the higher angels of our neocortex, we learn to unpack our own prejudicial suitcases, sort truth from consensus reality, and make considered personal choices. Free-ish will is a moment-by-moment practice requiring self-scrutiny. Since our sense of "ought," or just deserts, is nearly automatic, more like "growing a limb than sitting in Sunday school and learning about vices and virtues," as Marc Hauser notes, we're called on to examine our most intimate appendages. Which of your "oughts" are crippled, outdated, or just plain wrong? Which phantom limbs should you prune off your moralist structure in order for it to root more authentically? How do these "oughts" affect how we see ourselves, or how we ought to be, as opposed to who we are? While "oughts" are the glue of social arrangements, they are also sources of conflict, confusion, pain, self-loathing, restriction, and misapprehension, especially when we use them to maintain some inauthentic way of being.

I know a radical feminist attorney, for example, whose psychosexual needs refuse to line up with her politics. Publicly, she's a ferocious advocate of female rights, a tireless crusader for women's liberation, opposed to what she loathes as the "patriarchy," which means the male-dominated world as it exists today (and for which I, as a man, feel automatically guilty). But in private, this public crusader for female freedom is radically, hopelessly submissive, and attracted only to macho men. In bed, especially, she wants someone to show her who's the boss, by way of bondage, mean talk, and other erotic accoutrements.

Her "ought" and her "is" are out of synch; what she wants for other women, politically, is opposed to what she lusts for personally. This makes her crazy a lot of the time, and fills her with self-judgment and moral fear. She questions her own authenticity, the contradiction between her walk and her talk. This terrifically well-meaning woman really can't stand that *both are true* nor does she have a clue how to integrate her emotional needs with her public persona. Because of this ethical disconnect, my friend has been unable to have non-abusive, long-lasting relationships. *Sex and the City* as this may sound, her moral dilemma is a common one. Given the choice between her political activism and private needs, she would not hesitate to sacrifice the latter. But she'd like to have a relationship, too, if such intimacy did not interfere with what my friend—as a flagrant, knee-jerk, post-sixties partisan—believes to be right and wrong.

Desire and fear. What we *want* to want—and what we desire—are so often antithetical. Gut mind contradicts head mind, which contradicts groin mind, which leaves us all in a heap. Desire does not speak the language of ought; the sensual and the rational rarely mesh. The good news is that they can be brought closer together. Culturally acquired traits (such as political judgment) are easier to change than emotional and physical needs. Indeed, they have been shown to be malleable *within a single generation,* meaning that things like sexism and prejudice can actually be shifted when consensus reality makes room for such shifts. Nature has provided our moral organ with a great deal of leeway for the majority of choices that we make. Free-ish will can, indeed, change our oughts and elevate consciousness.

It's important to remember that we have a negativity bias, though. We are prepared by evolution for bad things to impact us more forcefully than good. As Haidt points out, "Our responses to threats and unpleasantness are faster, stronger, and harder to inhibit than responses to opportunities and pleasures." It's true. Haven't you ever wondered why, hours after you left the party, you're still obsessing over the single snob in a roomful of friends who wouldn't give you the time of day? Or why that nasty little voice inside your head is always predicting the very worst? Our brains are hardwired for threat and distrust. We place greater value on negative acts than positive ones. In one test, subjects suggested that it would take twenty-five acts of life-saving heroism to make up for a single murder. In marriage studies, spouses estimate that it takes five good deeds to make up for one lousy screwup. In Yiddish there's a saying that it takes twelve good men to build a house and one bad man to destroy it. It is easy in life to contaminate things but hard to purify.

The negativity bias can be a disaster when it comes to consensus reality. Cultural shifts with the faintest glimmer of innovation or envelope-pushing are often rejected for fear that they will lead to failure (you can't be too careful). We become stubborn in our negative predictions and refuse to consider alternative views. We bypass opportunities for change and open-mindedness. We're convinced that our way is the right one—full stop. Children go through this stage—the Terrible Twos—when every suggestion is met with a strident "No!" This is because children at that age are going through a phase when newly learned rules take on a kind of sacredness and unchangeability, a stage known as "immaculate justice." The budding ego is stomping its foot. As children become more sophisticated in their understanding of right and wrong, they gain moral flexibility. We hope.

Empathy deepens into kindness. We become people capable of altruism, automatic acts of nobility that contradict the negative bias. A child falls into a well. There's no time for "ought" or cost-benefit analysis, no time to think about reputation, self-protection, or common sense. There is simply the fact of needing to help. For a split second the suffering of another person passes before your eyes. Your mirror neurons go into gear. You feel the child's endangerment in your own body. Then you dive.

When the Penis Gets Hard,
the Brain Goes Soft

FEELING TRUMPS REASON MOST OF THE TIME, though the rational mind tells us differently. While humans may be *rationis capax*—endowed with unique powers of logic and discrimination—reason is a fairly weak instrument compared to the Stradivarius of our emotions. "Unlike walking, eating, or hearing, things we do easily, without instruction or education, reasoning is hard and requires experience and tutelage," Marc Hauser points out. When emotions flare, reason declines in proportion to passion; the more intense the feeling, the more ineffectual the rational mind becomes.

We are a wayward and willful species. A marked feature of our psychology is the inability to bring our motivation in line with what we know to be prudent. The design gap between reason and emotion has been called by psychologists "the enemy within." This flaw is deepened considerably when reason seeks its own reward. Motivated reasoning, meaning reason with an agenda, is among our worst ethical potholes. People who are motivated to reach a particular conclusion are the worst reasoners of all, we're told. Everyone knows how easy it is to find good reasons for doing what we know to be foolish, when blinding emotions pull us off track. We all know, intuitively, that just because we can make things add up on paper, or can calculate them *just so* in order to justify them, this doesn't mean they feel right or *are* right. Until the nineteenth century, to cite an obvious example, slavery was a defended custom. The need for slavery was justified by corresponding needs for labor, goods, and profit. Reasoning turned slavery into a necessary evil by making a case for greed, competitiveness, and selfishness as innate human traits. In this way, we reasoned our way *down* Jacob's ladder instead of up. It's hard not to notice that when actions are described as "only human," we're often rationalizing questionable behavior that we would rather not give up. This is how motivated reasoning can defeat us.

It's interesting to learn that irrationality comes with an upside. Not being strictly rational, we are able to be quick on our feet and flexible in changing environments. This is why evolution has shaped us to be predictably irrational. "An ape that in any circumstances conceives of a banana as the highest good will be at a constant disadvantage to a creature that is able to assess the importance of a banana depending on circumstances," one scientist quips. In human life, we're sometimes able to use intuition over reason to correct the story-making mind's tendency to become stuck in our own narratives. If people were never irrational, we could never surprise ourselves.

A disconnect exists between the story we tell ourselves *about* our own choices and how we are actually making them. Experiments in "moral dumbfounding" reveal the depths of our own ignorance about the choice-making apparatus, and who—or what—inside us is actually doing the choosing. Believing our own fiction, we recoil in horror and disbelief when our stories about motivation are popped like party balloons. In a famous series of experiments, subjects were asked about a one-time-only sexual fling between a brother and sister. Picture the scene. Angelina and James are traveling alone in Ibiza by sailboat under an ouzo moon. It's just the two of them, the stars, and sea—no one will know if anything sexual happens between them. They make a blood pact—only once, and never to be spoken of again. Angelina and James gird themselves with condoms and coils and tear off each other's dampened clothes. The lovemaking is everything they've dreamt of since playing on the swings together as children. No harm is done to either of them.

Should Angelina and James have taken a chill pill? Were they wrong to get into each other's pants? When asked this question, participants overwhelmingly voted yes—it was wrong for James to use Angelina like that (don't even *talk* about how she used him), without a shadow of doubt. When subjects were asked to explain why Angelina and James were such wicked siblings for going all the way, the volunteers offered an airtight reason: Incest is wrong, plain and simple. Disgust over in-family sex appeared to make wrongness a foregone conclusion. Participants grimaced and gagged with repulsion. When the researcher pressed these subjects yet again, they gave another reason: Incest is illegal and harmful to families. Reminded that nobody would ever know—and what people didn't know couldn't possibly hurt them—most test subjects just threw up their hands and said, "I judge it to be wrong because it makes me sick [angry, disgusted, outraged, et al.] and that's all there is to it."

This is what Haidt calls moral dumbfounding. We fully expect to find reasons justifying our limbic responses—in this case, that sibling lust is wrong—and seem perplexed when we can't. We're left scratching our heads, unable to explain our beliefs, *yet unmoved in our fundamental convictions.* That's the dangerous part about being half rational: Our gut beliefs are more or less impervious to reason. The mind makes a judgment call but does not reveal its operative principles. Instead, we give weak, frequently incoherent reasons to bolster judgments that are really just knee-jerk emotional responses. The story-making mind struggles heroically to weave experience into a self-justifying tale that we can deliver with confidence to others. This moral reasoning is, as Haidt describes it, "the press secretary for a secretive administration, constantly generating the most persuasive arguments it can muster for policies whose true origins and goals are unknown."

It's easy to make up disgusting, morally dumbfounding riddles. After the gross-out over Angelina and James, researchers suggested instances of a hungry family eating road kill, of wiping your toilet with the national flag, or having sex with a chicken carcass you're about to eat. Each of these scenarios drew big yucks and vomiting noises from the group, although subjects could not justify their disgust. Reason gets particularly muddled when passion assails us. Behavioral economist Dan Ariely used horny teenagers as test subjects to get to the bottom of where reason stopped. Across the board, he found that people's predictions about their own virtue were wildly overestimated. In response to five questions about their propensity to engage in questionable activities, such as unsafe sex, the youths' predictions—made in a cold rational state—were off by more than double (136 percent) once they were in a hot, aroused state. In a set of questions about using condoms, these teens were 25 percent more likely to predict they would forgo condoms in the aroused state than in the cold state. Across the nineteen questions about sexual preferences, their predicted desire to engage in a variety of "somewhat odd" sexual activities was nearly twice as high (72 percent higher) when aroused than cold. They largely failed to predict the influence of arousal on their sexual preferences, morality, and approach to safe sex. Prevention, protection, conservatism, and morality were tossed aside. They had been duped by reason into believing that they were more virtuous than they were.

Reason fools us with semantics as well. In another set of experiments, patients tended to choose certain medical treatments when told that 90 percent of those treated were still alive five years later, rather than that 10 percent were dead. The feelings aroused by thoughts of dying led them to reject an option that might have been beneficial. Language tricks, visual tricks, and logic tricks can all be used by our reasoning minds to cover up funky motives. We may overthink choices that we could make in an eye blink if we noticed how we actually *felt*.

Finally, it's impossible to talk about justice and fairness without mentioning the trolley problem. The trolley problem is to moral psychology what drooling dogs were to Ivan Pavlov.

Invented by an English philosopher named Philippa Foot, the trolley problem presents us with a dilemma that pits reason against emotion on a bridge overlooking a railway station. Walking home from work one day, you see a trolley car hurtling down a train track, the conductor slumped over the controls. In the path of the trolley are five men working on the track, oblivious to the danger. You're watching from a fork in the track and can pull a lever that will divert the trolley to the other track, saving the five men. Unfortunately, the trolley would then run over a single worker who is laboring on the spur. Is it permissible to throw the switch, killing one man to save five? When two hundred thousand people from a hundred countries were asked this question, almost everyone said yes.

Consider now a different scene. You're on the bridge overlooking the tracks and spot the runaway trolley bearing down on the five workers. This time, the only way to stop the trolley is to throw a heavy object into its path. The only heavy object around is the fat man standing next to you. Should you throw the fat man off the bridge?

Both dilemmas present you with the option of sacrificing one life to save five, and so, by the utilitarian standard of what would result in the greatest good for the greatest number, the two dilemmas are morally equivalent. But most people don't see it that way, because most people are not utilitarians at heart. We're empathizers. While the majority would agree to pull the impersonal switch in the first dilemma, most of them would *not* push the fat man to his death to save the same five workers. When pressed for a reason why one option is permissible but the other isn't, laboratory subjects unsurprisingly cannot come up with a coherent reason. They are morally dumbfounded. "It just *feels* wrong," they say, helpless to articulate why this is so. But it's not exactly rocket science. When people are involved, emotion kicks in. When emotions kick in, we make different choices. After shooting at an enemy in the Spanish Civil War, George Orwell couldn't finish off the job. "I did not shoot," the novelist later wrote. "I had come here to shoot at fascists but a man who is holding up his trousers isn't a 'fascist.' He is visibly a fellow creature, similar to yourself, and you don't feel like shooting him." Such "sympathy breakthroughs" are common among soldiers in wartime.

The Mardi Gras Effect

Humans everywhere maintain some system or other of fairness, rules, punishment, law, and reward. When wrong is done, punishment must be inflicted to make it right. Humans believe in just deserts, which relies on the idea that the world has a kind of moral equilibrium that must be maintained through reward and restitution. The values of our consensus reality are internalized as necessary for that equilibrium. This internalization creates the Freudian superego—better known as a conscience—which is generally pleased when we comply with society's ethics and unhappy when we don't. The reward centers of our brain, the nucleus accumbens and the caudate nucleus, fire up to thank us for playing fair.

But our sense of justice is derived from local custom, politics, prejudice, and tradition, which is why laws are sometimes ridiculous. In Connorsville, Wisconsin, a man is legally prohibited from shooting a gun while his female partner is having an orgasm. In California, it is a misdemeanor to shoot at any kind of game from a moving vehicle, unless the target is a whale. In New York City, it is actually illegal to shake a dust mop out a window. "Justice is at best a very distant ideal toward which different tribes aspire, moving by various, circuitous, and culturally determined routes," as one writer puts it. The history of violence in the world is the history of incompatible ideals of justice clashing against one another. Each side believes in its own version of the just world hypothesis, which posits that people get what they deserve. But what they deserve isn't altogether clear. Though little evidence of this "just world" exists, our moral organ requires this idealized notion of balance to help us make sense of things, avoid chaos, and maintain a sense of control. The trouble is that believing people get what they deserve, and deserve what they get, often leads to blaming the victims of tragedies and exonerating those whom the courtroom favors. The illusion of justice is too often enough.

It is the arbitrary nature of customs and laws that keeps lawyers rich, penitentiaries full, and ethics columnists busy at newspapers. We need help untangling the knots of personal interpretation. Mostly, these quandaries don't have to do with major violations— very few of us are contemplating murder, grand larceny, or the torture of innocents—but instead center on minor moral infractions. We sweat the small stuff because it's the hardest. We torment ourselves over small-scale rules because those are the ones that city hall can monkey around with and tell us it's fair because they said so. "The rules of equity or justice depend entirely on the particular state and condition in which men are placed, and owe their origin and existence to that utility," Hume explains.

Which brings us to another conundrum. Do we obey laws that are patently unfair in hopes of remaining good citizens, or follow the dictates of conscience outside the walls of local opprobrium? As the Milgram experiment famously proved, obedience can be ghastly. Begun at Yale University in 1961, three months after the start of the trial of Nazi war criminal Adolf Eichmann in Jerusalem, Stanley Milgram's experiment was devised to answer the question: "Eichmann and his million accomplices in the Holocaust were just following orders; are we right in calling them accomplices?" His findings stunned the world. A full 65 percent of the participants in the Milgram experiment were willing to inflict a maximum electrical shock of 450 volts to innocent people, despite their screams, simply because they were told to do so by an authority figure.

Then the infamous Stanford prison experiment went even further. In 1971, psychologist Philip Zimbardo designed an experiment to demonstrate how situational authority and power could make good people do sickening things. Two dozen men were recruited to participate in what they were told would be a two-week prison simulation. Predominantly white and middle class, these men had been deemed psychologically stable before the experiment began. A mock jail was built in the basement of Stanford's Jordan Hall. Zimbardo would play the superintendent. The men playing guards were provided with a weapon—a wooden baton—and a uniform. They were given mirrored sunglasses to prevent eye contact. Participants who'd chosen to play the part of prisoners were "arrested" at their homes and charged with armed robbery. The local Palo Alto police department assisted Zimbardo with the arrests and conducted full booking procedures on the prisoners, which included fingerprints and mug shots. Then the captives were transported to the mock prison where they were strip-searched and given their new identity: serial numbers. Prisoners were forced to wear ill-fitting smocks and stocking caps. Guards called prisoners by their assigned numbers, which were sewn on their uniforms. A chain around their ankles reminded them of their role as prisoners. During a pre-arrest orientation, the guards were told that they could not physically harm the prisoners but they could use intimidation and fear to make prisoners feel powerlessness.

The experiment quickly grew out of hand, as Zimbardo

recounts in his book *The Lucifer Effect*. Almost immediately, the guards' protocol began to break down. After prisoners rebelled on the second day, the guards grew increasingly cruel. (A full one-third of them were described later as exhibiting genuine sadistic tendencies.) There were physical assaults by guards; some prisoners were forced to go nude, à la Abu Ghraib, and to simulate homosexual sex. Guards shot prisoners with fire extinguishers and allowed sanitary conditions to decline. Some prisoners were prevented from relieving themselves while others could not empty their sanitation buckets. Zimbardo concluded the experiment early—angering most of the guards—when a student of his, Christina Maslach (whom he later married), objected to the appalling conditions of the prison. It's not surprising that a woman put a screeching halt to this testosterone-fest. Of the fifty outside persons who had seen the prison, Maslach was the only one who questioned its morality, Zimbardo later admitted. After only six days instead of the planned two weeks, the Stanford Prison Experiment was shut down.

How does something like this happen? Can a riding crop and pair of mirrored sunglasses really turn a good person bad? The answer is yes—and no. We know that we have a tendency to overestimate our own character strength while underestimating the power of situations. This has something to do with forgetting that our personal identities are socially situated. "We are *where* we live, eat, work, and make love," Zimbardo has written. Although you probably think of yourself as having a consistent personality across time and space, this is simply untrue. You are not the same person at home as you are at the office; trundling through Macy's or making love; drinking with friends or lost and alone in a foreign city. Moving from one situation to another, one role to the next, we adjust our definition of right and wrong. Please read the previous sentence twice. In a book called *Snakes in Suits,* Paul Babiak and Robert Hare remind us that "many traits that may be desirable in a corporate context, such as ruthlessness, lack of social conscience, and single-minded devotion to success, would be considered psychopathic outside of it." We make these mercurial character adjustments with frightening ease. Our values and behavior can be altered by anything from plastic surgery to changing our name, from joining a new religion to taking an online alias, joining a gang, or moving to a different neighborhood.

That's how malleable, and how surgically alterable, moral identity can be. Americans, in particular, like to think of ourselves as rugged individualists with characters hewn from Wyoming granite, but we're actually more like Play-Doh. The discovery of mirror neurons alone is enough to demolish the myth of a constant, unwavering self. We play different roles throughout our lives. Our roles have different parameters. We adjust the definitions of right and wrong, injecting different characters into different situations. Just look at Tony Soprano. When Tony says it's "just business"—making some enemy "sleep with the fishes"—we almost believe him. Tony tells us it's nothing personal, really, as he throws the body into the river. Sitting at home in front of the TV set, does anyone really hate Tony Soprano? Of course not. He suffers up there on his mobster throne (those therapy scenes can be killers), and, besides, his long-suffering wife, Carmela, is such a sweetheart. Murder turns into good TV.

This is because we compartmentalize. Compartmentalization is what allows us to play different roles and act like different people in different circumstances. There are four ways that we can disengage morally from destructive or evil things we do, four methods of compartmentalization. We can (1) reframe our behavior as virtuous; (2) distance ourselves from the harm we inflict by minimizing personal responsibility; (3) change the way we think about the harm itself; or (4) blame the victims or deem them unworthy of humane treatment. Most of us have employed all of these evasion tactics at one time or other. In situations where the cognitive controls that usually guide socially acceptable behavior are blocked, suspended, or distorted, conscience seems to fizzle out. Anonymity is especially enticing and dangerous; any setting that hides people's identities, including virtual reality, tends to reduce our sense of personal responsibility, care, and decorum. Just try putting on a mask. If you've never hidden your face in public, you're missing a chance to know your demons. Remember the moment in *Lord of the Flies* when Jack covers himself with war paint and screams with delight at his own reflection?

> He looked in astonishment, no longer at himself but at an awesome stranger. He spilt the water and leapt to his feet, laughing excitedly. Beside the pool his sinewy body held up a mask that drew their eyes and appalled them. He began to dance and his laughter became a bloodthirsty snarling. He capered toward Bill, and the mask was a thing on its own, behind which Jack hid, liberated from shame and self-consciousness.

Changing appearance can open doors to our contradictory nature. The mask can sometimes make the man. Zimbardo describes how our Dionysian impulses of lust and uninhibited release are pitted against Apollonian traits of constraint, reason, and social conformity. "Dionysus was the god of drunkenness, the god of insanity, the god of sexual frenzy and battle lust," he wrote after the Stanford Prison Experiment. "Dionysus's dominion includes all states of being that entail loss of self-awareness and rationality, the suspension of linear time, and the abandonment of the self to those urges in human nature that overthrow codes of behavior and public reaponsibility."

If you've been to Mardi Gras in New Orleans, you've seen this demonic force at play. Anything goes on Bourbon Street on a hot afternoon in February. I once saw a pair of half-naked leather queens rolling around on the sidewalk, spanking each other with enormous glee while a half-bored French Quarter cop on horseback sat there joking with a group of bible belt tourists, powdered ladies in candy-colored pantsuits holding up their stinking drunk husbands. It was tragic, brilliant, and terrifying from an ethical standpoint. These good Christian folks wouldn't condone a homosexual marriage if their eternal lives depended on it. But on Bourbon Street on a hot afternoon, with three beers under their belts before lunch, who the hell cared? Smack that bottom! Lick that boot! Stick that where the sun don't shine! They had abandoned their scruples along with their Samsonites back at the Super 8.

Situational power takes hold of us in new situations where we have no recall of previous guidelines for behavior. Removed from our familiar context, where the reward structures are different and expectations are violated, our personalities cannot function according to results from past experiences. Deprived of ethical reference points, we're unable to predict what matters and what doesn't. In situations where we do have a role to play, with reliable boundaries circumscribing what is appropriate, expected, and reinforced in a given setting, the values that guide us in normal mode can hold sway. Compartmentalization allows us to sort conflicting aspects of our behavior into different mental "role baskets" that do not spill into one another. This is how a "good husband can . . . be a guiltless adulterer; a saintly priest can then be a lifelong pederast; a kindly farmer can then be a heartless slave master," Zimbardo notes. We use roles to absolve ourselves of guilt. Overestimating our reasoning powers, and underestimating the force of situations, we're frequently surprised by our own extreme contradictions. We oversimplify our own complexity and construct imaginary, seemingly impermeable boundaries between good and evil, us and them, the damned and the saved, the straight and the not straight. But this illusion of opposites sets us up for a fall. Believing ourselves immune to situational forces, we let down our guard and fall prey to unexpected ulterior impulses.

It's wise to bear this closely in mind. It's helpful to be aware that our personalities have movable parts, and that some situations are simply more powerful than our inconstant "self" can manage. Sophie has to make a choice, sometimes; we're frequently outgunned by life. I know a woman who, while hiding from Nazi soldiers in a Polish basement, was forced to choose between sacrificing herself, and fifteen others, or smothering her own baby daughter. She was trapped, the SS were in the house, the weeks-old infant was crying, and this group of terrified Jews was moments away from being discovered. She put a pillow over her baby's face. This brave woman survived the war, and lived to see her three other children grow up, marry, and give her a slew of beautiful grandchildren. Was she wrong to sacrifice one life for fifteen? Was she evil for doing what she did? Or was this woman a hero? Did the dog-eat-dog reality of war change what good meant—or could mean? What sacrifice could be more agonizing than a mother's for her child? Was she noble or was she a murderer? Or was she, as I would suggest, both? For the Inuits, and some other cultures, infanticide is morally permissible. They justify the killing of children on the grounds of limited resources. To allow these children to live would infringe on their own ethic of care.

Suckers, Grudgers,
and Cheaters

O N   A   L I G H T E R   N O T E, my college girlfriend was the
Robin Hood of women's lingerie. Laura had a PhD in
Renaissance literature, spoke four languages fluently, and took no
greater pleasure in life than stealing overpriced panties and peeka-
boo nighties from the dressing room at Macy's. Aside from her
weakness for shoplifting, Laura was otherwise straight as an arrow.
What's more, her quirky ethics were strict and clear: She would rip
off only department stores—never a mom-and-pop place—and
never more often than once a month. Twice a month would have
been excessive, she insisted. Her tendencies were excessive and illegal already, of course, but I didn't have the heart to say so. I enjoyed
the bedroom perks too much.

Evolution prepared us humans to be devious, self-serving, and
only half-honest, inclined to grab the lion's share of goodies without being thrown out of the group. Homo sapiens became wired for
truthfulness only to the extent that it suited us, pleased others, and
preserved our reputations. We are willing to break rules to benefit
ourselves but only within limits we can justify. We are good and fair,

most of the time—at least in our own minds—but that doesn't exactly make us straight shooters. The world is a hard place, we tell ourselves. Our internal cop stops us only when we contemplate big transgressions. As long as we're not pigs, we believe, it's okay to bend the rules. I'm not averse to stealing a handful of nuts from the A&P, though I'd never swipe anything in a box. We walk off with ashtrays from hotel rooms but wouldn't pocket crystal from somebody's house. The superego worries over our reputation and what others think about our integrity. But that rarely includes stray cashews and junk from hotels. Small dishonesties bypass our ethical radar; our impartial spectator doesn't give a hoot. We're more honest when status or reputation are involved, however; cooperation levels skyrocket during game theory experiments in which players know one another. But even when there's no chance of being caught, studies show, most people still don't contemplate grand larceny.

Suckers, grudgers, and cheaters inhabit every human society. Suckers are gullible or overly generous people with a habit of being taken advantage of. Grudgers are individuals with a particular taste for punishment and harboring resentment, sometimes long after forgiveness is called for. And cheaters are, well, cheaters—freeloaders, advantage takers, the exceptional case to every rule. Cheaters range from habitual low-level rule benders to Machiavellian sociopaths who obey the law of the jungle, where the most heartless, ambitious, disloyal, duplicitous, and selfish win, no matter how they do it.

Our ability to detect cheaters requires logical inference and the ability to read emotion. Our carefully tuned moral apparatus enables us to pick up signs of deception, mostly through nonverbal cues, such as inconsistencies of voice or expression. The ability to detect "nonreciprocators"—the small percentage of people in any group who'll always attempt to exploit others for their own gain—is among our most primitive design features. This evaluative machinery is more powerful when we have a personal stake in outcomes; subjects' performances in cheater detection studies improve dramatically when there is a payoff for finding the violation. Because trust is required for cooperation, no commodity is more valuable than trustworthiness in the survival game. In biblical times, men swore oaths by placing a hand under one another's loins (the words "testify," "testimony," and "testicle" share a common Latin root) to show they were serious.

Whether you're a hunter-gatherer living on the savanna, or an executive on Wall Street, your brain is running particular software for social contracts, precautions, and punishment for group-undermining behavior. We do this via an "exchange organ" in the brain that keeps track of fairness—not a literal organ but different neurons and tissues working together to do a single job. Determinations of right and wrong are based on tallies made by this exchange organ of favors received and given, generosity compensated or not, status attained or refused: the arithmetic of perceived personal justice.

For trust to be established, four criteria for cooperation must be met. There must be (1) an overlap in desires; (2) a chance of future encounters with the same individual; (3) a memory of past encounters with that individual; and (4) a value associated with future outcomes. Sympathy prompts a person to offer a favor. Anger protects another from dealing with a cheater who won't reciprocate, punishing the ingrate with indignation. Gratitude impels a beneficiary to reward those who help him, while guilt prompts cheaters in danger of discovery to make amends. Studies show that our brains respond differently to offers perceived as fair versus unfair, and that the outcome of an exchange is predicted by the state of our brain right before making the decision. This is useful information. When we're angry, we tend to reject. When we're reasonable, we're likely to negotiate. So long as a favor helps the recipient more than it costs the giver, and the recipient returns the favor when fortunes reverse, cooperation can continue.

But you have to factor in selfishness. We believe what we want to believe. Egocentrism shapes our ideas about fairness, as it does about moral life, generally. Fair is what we *like*. We overestimate our own contributions and underestimate the contributions of others. People consider a minor unfairness to themselves as worse than a major unfairness that happens to someone else. Since most interactions in nature are zero-sum games where one party wins and the other loses, and selfishness cannot be avoided, our exchange organ evolved to protect us from others' dishonesty. When we detect cheaters, we become vengeful; when we're treated fairly, gratitude helps to seal the deal, bonding us more deeply with allies and promoting further reciprocation. Guilt helps to chasten a dishonest nature. Reciprocity remains accepted. Ingrates tend to be left in the cold.

Through personal bias, we view fairness in a descending hierarchy of merit as it becomes more distant from us, from closest kin to sworn enemies. We have two kinds of genes for altruism: those for kin and those targeted toward outsiders. Kin selection makes us sensitive to the suffering and needs of close kin, while reciprocal altruism connects us to those who live outside our inner circle. It's more or less okay (maybe not *okay*, but tolerable) to not give money to a stranger begging in the street. "If that beggar is a member of your family, the judgment is entirely different. If parents starve their children to death, this is generally described as 'killing.' Yet, if the same people were to pass by a starving beggar, knowing that he might die without food, this would be called 'allowing him to die,'" as philosopher Shelly Kagan points out.

The distinction between right and wrong shifts on this fluctuating ego-based scale. But the underlying rule is the same: reciprocity. It's golden. If you've ever listened to Indian music and know that steady *shadja* beat underneath the dancing notes of the raga, you might compare that consistent, unifying movement to how reciprocity works in our lives. We are master reciprocators as a species; back and forth exchange is our natural mode. We reciprocate even when it's not necessary. In a famous study involving Christmas cards sent by strangers, an unexpectedly high percentage of recipients returned the favor, just to be nice. Sleazy salespeople exploit the reciprocal response with freebies, suckering us into buying things we don't need. The dark side of reciprocity is revenge. All schoolchildren learn, as Auden reminds us in his poem "September 1, 1939," that "those to whom evil is done/do evil in return."

Neither kin altruism nor reciprocity completely explains the extraordinary degree to which people cooperate with strangers they'll never meet again, and sacrifice for large groups composed of non-kin, moral psychologists tell us. We are fair in the vast majority, to our own minds, most of the time, with everyone. But where does your circle stop? Where does compassion conk out? At what point does "us" become "them" for you; where do you start to look away? Does your circle end with your family, your nation, your color, your faith, your sexuality, or your species? Are animals worthy of ethical treatment or do they, as wantons, become our objects? This question is worth asking because we are capable of extending our empathic range. "The higher an animal has risen in the stages of evolution, the less is the weight of stereotyped behavior patterns that are strictly determined," Erich Fromm reminds us. The more highly evolved the animal, in other words, the more freely it can make its own choices, push its own ethical circumference.

Reciprocal altruism allows cooperative networks to expand outside family, state, and nation. Societies ruled by kin selection tend to be nepotistic, narrow-minded, and isolationist. Those ruled by reciprocal altruism have far greater possibilities. Still, all relationships need care and attention, and reconciliations after breaches of conduct become all the more important outside the protection of family forgiveness. In the same way that birds rebuild their nests, and spiders are forever mending their webs, our primate ancestors learned that reconciliation was key to protecting the woof and warp of social fabric.

The Green-Eyed Monsters

ENVY AND GREED ARE OUR NEMESES. We are naturally drawn to reciprocity but prefer to come out way ahead. We want not only what's necessary in order to survive, but more of everything. Gnawing at the desire to be good is the temptation to be obscenely self-serving. Anthropologists tell us that hunters and gatherers tended to be far more egalitarian than the agriculturalists who followed them (farming made the storage and accumulation of homegrown food and livestock not only possible but highly desirable). With the development of capitalism, greed became a form of implicit virtue for enterprising citizens, and we've grown only more competitive and mercenary with increased industrialization fed by the massive, ravening hierarchies of dollar-hungry corporations. Greed's verdant-eyed cousin, envy, is also epidemic in a culture where until recently (especially in America) the official motto was the bigger the better, and more is more. I've heard it suggested that not since before the fall of the Roman Empire has there been such a culture-wide obsession with *stuff*. And the Romans didn't have QVC.

The feeding frenzy encouraged by our addiction-fueling media has helped to create our modern sense of emptiness needing to be filled. Religious scholar Andrew Harvey described this self-defeating system to me a few years back:

> This culture feeds off an anxiety and depression that it carefully nurtures with a consumer machine that needs to keep us greedy to keep going. It is highly organized, versatile and sophisticated: it assaults us from every angle with its propaganda, and creates an almost impregnable environment of addiction around us . . . Obsessed with hopes, dreams and ambitions which promise happiness but lead only to misery, we are like people crawling through an endless desert, dying of thirst, and all this culture holds out to us is a drink of salt water, designed to make us thirstier.

This reminds me of the Buddhist notion of the Hungry Ghost. Hungry Ghosts are those starving figures in Buddhist mythology (metaphors for the insatiable ego) condemned to eternal craving in a world of elusive satisfactions. Nothing is ever enough for these monsters. There exists no end to their craving for more. But it is the greed of the Hungry Ghost that is desecrating the face of our planet. Environmentalists like Bill McKibben have been warning us against our rapacious selves for decades. A few years back, McKibben found himself standing in Beijing's Tiananmen Square, gazing up toward the sun in the sky—and not being able to find it—when he had a scary revelation about culture envy and conspicuous consumption.

"You could stare straight at the sun if you could even figure out where in the sky it was," McKibben told me when we spoke. "I was in complete shock." Doing the math, he estimated that by the year 2031, barring natural disaster or mass contraception, there would be roughly 1.3 billion Chinese as well off as their American counterparts. "If the Chinese owned cars like we do, they would add 1.1 billion cars to the eight hundred million already on the road," McKibben said. "If the Chinese ate meat the way we do, they would consume two thirds of the food on the planet. The earth simply could not support that.

"People are understanding just where the culture of greed got us," McKibben went on. "It's as if we've done a controlled experiment to see if materialism as a path to happiness works and found it doesn't. For all our material progress, all the billions of barrels of oil and millions of acres of trees that it took to create it, we have not moved the satisfaction meter an inch." It is well known that alcoholism, suicide, and depression rates have skyrocketed in direct proportion to our affluence. Today's average American child reports suffering higher levels of anxiety than the average child *under psychiatric care* in the 1950s. The *New York Times* recently reported on a 2007 UNICEF study of the well-being of children in twenty-one developed countries that ranked American youth second from the bottom.

In China, McKibben ran straight into America's shadow, in the person of an eighteen-year-old factory worker named Liu Xian. He and the girl strike up a conversation, which he describes in his book *Deep Economy*. McKibben told Liu Xian that he had noticed how many of the girls in the factory dorm had stuffed animals on their beds and asked her if she had one like everyone else. "Her eyes filled ominously," he writes. "She liked them very much, she said, but she had to save all her earnings for her future." Later, when he brought a stuffed dog to the factory, Liu Xian and her fellow workers "were as pleased as [he'd] ever seen a person." The disconnect between the Chinese girl's gratitude and his own daughter's material underwhelm ("Her room boasts a density of Beanie Babies") still affects him. How could a stuffed animal possibly have the same meaning for her? he asks about his daughter. This is why Liu Xian's story continues to haunt him. "In that world, possessions still deliver," McKibben writes. "Any solution we consider [for redistributing wealth] must contain some answer to her tears."

Country rocker Will Oldham says it another way: "It is more rewarding to be complicit with scarcity than excess." But have you ever not bought a single thing because its production was based in China, or some other worker-suppressed Third World nation? Unlikely. Most of us are too envious of others' possessions to voluntarily do without ourselves. Indeed, envy is one of our more fascinating moral emotions. "Envy is the great leveler," according to writer Dorothy Sayers. "If it cannot level things up, it will level them down. Rather than have anyone happier than itself, it will see us all miserable together."

Envy, which is tied to spite, is a universal emotion that nevertheless causes shame and embarrassment when we recognize it in ourselves. Envy has received far less critical attention than its nasty relative, jealousy. Where envy is triggered by an inequity, or disparity in the possession of valued resources, jealousy is triggered when one individual is threatened by another. "Central to the emotion of envy is its clandestinity, its surreptitiousness," Joseph Epstein wrote in his book *Envy*. "People confident of their religion . . . say envy is owing to Original Sin, part of the baggage checked through on the way out of the Garden of Eden." For a long time, it was believed that envy served no moral purpose. But moral philosophers now say that this is false. Ethnographic literature on hunter-gatherers suggests that envy is central to our aspiration for just deserts, "motivating achievement, serving the conscience of self and other, and alerting us to inequities that, if fueled, can lead to escalated violence," as Hauser puts it. Schadenfreude, the cold-hearted pleasure we take in another's failures, may also have been a survival tool. The satisfaction of bitter gloating could prevent violence and further discord. We wave our schadenfreude like an honor flag when we see the terribly guilty punished; we cheer at the spectacle of Bernard Madoff being hauled off to the pen after ruining the financial lives of thousands. The trouble is that our taste for schadenfreude can corrupt our justice systems. "The infliction of cruelty with a clear conscience is a delight to moralists. That is why they invented hell," Bertrand Russell noted sadly.

Hell found a colony of kindred spirits among the primitive East African people known as the Ik, made famous by Colin Turnbull in his book *The Mountain People*. Through starvation, the Ik had deteriorated to the point of dehumanization. Schadenfreude veered into outright cruelty. Harm to children was not exempted. "Men would watch a child with eager anticipation as it crawled towards the fire, then burst into gay and happy laughter as it plunged a skinny hand into the coals," Turnbull reported. The anthropologist never saw children more than three years old being fed by adults, and observed that people ate away from their homes so as to avoid having to share their food. It was common practice to pry open the mouths of old people to retrieve food they had not yet swallowed. Hunger appears to have robbed the Ik of human decency itself.

But life in extremis does not always run this foul course. Bitter circumstances can prompt elevated behavior even in the most tormenting places. Think of Viktor Frankl, the father of logotherapy, writing this after years spent in Nazi detention:

[We] who lived in the concentration camps can remember the men who walked through the huts comforting others, giving away their last piece of bread. They may have been few in number but they offer sufficient proof that everything can be taken away from a man but one thing: the last of the human freedoms—to choose one's attitude, to choose one's own way. Every day, every hour, you [made] a decision which determined whether you would or would not submit to those powers which threaten to rob you of your very self, your inner freedom . . . Whether or not you would become the plaything of circumstance, renouncing freedom and dignity.

Even among the Ik, Turnbull found the embers of goodness past. An old woman to whom he'd given food suddenly burst into tears. She told him that it made her long for the good old days "when people had been kind to one another." With no better provisions at hand, we may be fed by memories of benevolence.

Lex Talionis

WOMEN TEND TO GRAVITATE toward connection while men have a greater taste for revenge. Studies show that men enjoy retribution more than women do. Still, both sexes adhere to the ancient law of blood spilt calling for blood spilling. After the Battle of Glen Fruin, in the Highlands of Scotland in 1603, sixty widows of the slain Colquhoun clansmen famously rode on white horses before King James VI, each carrying a stake displaying the bloody shirt of her husband, demanding revenge. "Waving the bloody shirt is an ancient semaphore that signals the passage, from one generation to the next, of the obligation for revenge," Lance Morrow writes. "The ancient laws of Ireland made a distinction between 'necessary murder' (which was either unpremeditated, done in self-defense, or to exact revenge) and 'unnecessary murder' (done for motives of gain)." Beyond the familiar idea of necessary evil lies the landscape of permissible evil—which has become the world's functioning workaday policy of evil, the framework within which we operate as a practical matter. "Permissible evil is the evil we can live with," Morrow tells us.

One measure of a civilization's progress is the distance it creates between aggrieved individuals and the administration of their need for vindication. We intervene in the path of revenge as part of a socially self-monitoring organism. Apparently, our struggle to rein in vengefulness has been the hallmark of each stage in the development of civilization. Governments learned from the beginning that unless forceful laws were made by the state, individuals would take it upon themselves to exact revenge for moral outrage. "When punishment does not at least approximate giving satisfaction to the victims of crime, and to those in the community who wish to demonstrate their moral outrage, these individuals will take it upon themselves to exact punishment (which will lead to) an escalation of private vendettas," philosopher Alan Goldman tells us. *Lex talionis*—an eye for an eye—fosters brutality. Take the case of Tyrone Thompson. A double murderer who served thirty-eight years in prison, Thompson was released in 2003 and now works at a Harlem facility for troubled youth, where I met him. Tyrone looks like a supersized Bill Cosby. At six foot four, with bulging muscles and perfectly capped teeth, he looks younger than his sixty-four years, and not at all like the kind of person who'd slash three men's throats in broad daylight, killing two of them, and feel no remorse whatever. "I felt good," he tells me matter-of-factly. "I did what I had to do."

Like a lot of people who kill for justice, Tyrone lived outside the conventional bounds of the law. He was a drug-involved adolescent in Harlem with a particular talent for cutting heroin. This was a rare and lucrative gift in the narcotics world. It made a fatherless teen like Tyrone, responsible for supporting his mother and grandmother, a wealthy boy in just a few years. It wasn't his first choice for a career—he would have preferred playing pro football—but cutting drugs after school was putting food on their kitchen table. It was also making him a big man in the neighborhood, snappily dressed and popular with the ladies.

"I was the shit!" Tyrone says with a chuckle, shaking his head in a boy-was-I-dumb kind of way. He kicks back in his office chair and puts his size-fourteen shoes on the desk. "I had respect in that world—not that it means much—but it meant something to me. I never wanted to hurt anybody."

"You were dealing heroin," I say.

"I was *cutting* it. Other people were selling it. Not that it excuses what I did, but let's keep the facts straight." Tyrone talks like somebody who's spent most of his life nitpicking the legal system. "Anyway, I was in the wrong place at the wrong time." His reputation in the neighborhood, and the profits he flaunted, got him on the bad side of a rival gang who decided that he would be better off dead. The gang put a hit out on him and one night, while drinking in a bar, Tyrone was clubbed over the head with a baseball bat, which left him paralyzed and comatose for three months. "When I woke up, I had to learn to walk again. I was seventeen years old. I would have left that life right then and there," he tells me. "Only these same bastards showed up at the house and threatened my family. My mama and grandma were scared to death."

"Did they know how you were earning money?"

"I'm not proud of it. Yeah, I think they knew. My grandma tried to set me straight, made me go to church with her. But I was young and greedy and liked my status. I promised them it wouldn't be forever. Anyway," Tyrone says, waving through the office window at a group of teenage boys whom he mentors, "I knew what I had to do."

Tyrone asked a couple of hooker friends to lure his enemies to a certain house in the neighborhood. He describes the scene: waiting in the bushes outside for their sign, entering the house with a butcher knife, finding one guy upstairs in a bedroom and slashing his throat, finding a second, then a third, and knifing them repeatedly. He reports this to me without any telling emotion in his voice. His task complete, Tyrone left the men for dead and hid out for a few months down in the Carolinas with family, waiting for the incident to blow over. One afternoon, investigators from the New York Police Department showed up on his doorstep and arrested him.

"Turns out one of the guys didn't die," Tyrone says, rolling his eyes. "I'd sliced his vocal chords but he was still alive. He ratted me out and that's how they found me."

"What were you thinking when you did it?" I ask.

"I wasn't thinking," he says. "These guys had tried to hurt my family. What choice did I have?" The answer seems self-evident to Tyrone. "I felt cold as ice but my mind went red. There was no way I could control it. These guys crossed a line and they had to die. I knew what I had to do," he repeats.

"No remorse?"

"You don't get it," he says, making a prayer gesture with his hands. Tyrone means white folks like me, I think. "You people live in a different world. Where I come from, if you snitch to the cops, you're a dead man. Doesn't matter if you're right or not. Bring the law in and you're the traitor. Also, I would have been arrested. Who'd support my family then?"

For a moment, there's an awkward silence.

"I done my time," he says finally. "I'm clean and sober for eighteen years. I'm good with my God."

My eyes must have popped. "I'm not proud of what I done," he says, leaning forward in his chair, "but my God knows I didn't go looking for this. I didn't get joy out of killing two men. I'm not what you call a natural-born killer." He considers this and shakes his head. "I was never one of those guys."

Revenge seems to obviate contrition; Tyrone showed no remorse at all, and this absence of emotional consequence is disturbing. Forgiveness requires some proof of repentance—more than merely serving your time. From an early age, children can assess guilt according to visible signs of remorse. Asked to rate "badness" in the photographed faces of guilty people, most six-year-olds—and all eight-year-olds—rated a smiling face worse than a sad face (four-year-olds made no such distinction).

The absence of contrition amounts to the absence of an internal self-punishment system, a red flag indicating some serious moral lack in the offender. Juries seeking justice (which may be interpreted as local, codified, legal revenge) attempt to determine who's sorry and who's not. Unfortunately, our justice system operates on Old Testament principles. Vengeful justice systems create rules intended to reinforce their own dominance. We exact revenge on criminals by subjecting them to inhumane prison systems that create as much violence as they prevent. Already, experiments are being done in what's called "restorative justice," including alternative approaches to criminal rehab: enlightened strategies aimed at rehabilitating criminals rather than dehumanizing them. The government of Saudi Arabia has an innovative system for rehabilitating prisoners released from Guantánamo. Recognizing that a happily employed ex-jihadist is less likely to contemplate martyrdom, the Saudi system treats released prisoners like lost souls (instead of evil incarnate), educates them, settles them in government-provided homes, gives them a free automobile, and helps them find jobs. Of the nearly three hundred men returned to Saudi Arabia from Guantánamo, only eleven are known to have returned to terrorist activity (though figures are higher for prisoners returned to other countries).

When we realize just how hardwired *lex talionis* is in us, we become aware that our policing systems themselves need policing. Attempting to create a just society by inflicting emotional and physical violence is morally absurd. An improved penal system might allow prisoners to be productive and profitable while serving their time. This would be a win-win for bankrupted prison systems filled to overflowing with bored-stiff inmates.

Ends and Means

THE REFUSAL TO INFLICT VIOLENCE as a way of ending violence remains the minority view and requires
moral maturity. It requires that we examine our own taste for
revenge before passing judgment on others. History is full of good
people replicating the evil they seek to punish. This is why victim
types can be so ballistic; they play by their own victim-justified
rules. Indeed, "the psychology of the victim in an age of globalized
nuclear arms has become one of the greatest dangers in history,"
Morrow warns. One man's fair revenge is another man's atrocity.
One group's necessary evil is another country's genocide.

The principle of *double effect* is another loophole in this knit-
ting together of ends and means. According to this principle, otherwise prohibited acts may be justified if the harm they cause is not
intentional and the act's foreseeable and intended good effects out-
weigh its foreseeable bad effects. How's that for ambiguous, subjective, and unverifiable? Factoring in relationship obligations and
social bias, the principle of double effect may well become an ethical
mishmash. Remember that our sense of personal propriety operates

according to what we *believe* our intentions to be, not necessarily what they *are* (factoring in denial and self-deception). Similarly, our sense of just deserts—and what ends are justified by which means—depends on our interpretation of what others have done and not simply on objective data. It's fascinating to learn that in a study of people thinking about honesty and fairness, the only deterrent to deception was a subject's looking at himself in a mirror as he spoke. When we actually observe our own faces, we are less able to deceive ourselves. We have more trouble justifying ourselves *to* ourselves when faced with our own reflection. Hypocrisy, like addiction, is a condition that thrives on the denial of its own existence.

Most of us are engaged in impression management most of the time. Think of how many times a day you catch yourself worrying about how you're being seen, in contexts ranging from the office to the bedroom to the nursery. Think of how seamlessly you change, and how much time you spend pretending to be someone you're not in order to be loved, paid, laid, or esteemed. We tell "lies of perception" every day, subtle ones and big fat whoppers, in the process of social hologramming. There's a talented Mr. Ripley inside all of us who's busy nipping, tucking, and editing the image we wish to project in the world in exchange for what we want. Some people are more dissembling than others but all of us do it a little—like cheating. We may be secretly guilt-ridden over our own double effects, wondering how we can pretend to be so many people. We don't realize that this role changing is actually facilitated by which ethical tier—the particular level of right and wrong—we choose to stand on.

To better understand our own shifting standards, let's consider the textbook case of a gentleman dying of a rare disease. Better known as the Heinz dilemma, I prefer to use a more interesting sounding person called Astrid. There is only one drug that can save Astrid's dying husband, according to his doctors. Unfortunately, the drug is expensive to make and the woman who invented it (who happens to live in the same town) is charging ten times what it actually costs her to produce it. Astrid goes to everyone she knows to borrow the money but can only come up with one thousand dollars. Astrid tells the druggist that her husband is dying and begs her to sell the medicine at a reasonable price. The druggist refuses. Desperate, Astrid breaks into the druggist's supply closet and steals the precious drug for her dying husband.

Should Astrid have stolen the drug? There's a whole range of means and ends justification we can use to crack this ethical nut. These stages correspond to maturing levels of ethical awareness (first codified by psychologist Lawrence Kohlberg), but all remain within our repertoire throughout our lives. Regardless of our age, we retain the ability to tap into any of these options, depending on mood or circumstance:

- Stage One: *Obedience.* Astrid should not steal the medicine because she'll be thrown into jail, and that will mean that she's a bad person.
- Stage Two: *Self-interest.* Astrid should steal the medicine because she will be much happier if she saves her husband, even if she has to serve a prison sentence. (Or: Astrid should not steal the medicine because prison is miserable and she might suffer more in a jail cell than over her husband's death.)
- Stage Three: *Conformity.* Astrid should steal the medicine because she wants to be a good wife and her husband expects it. (Or: Astrid should not steal the drug because stealing is bad and she is not a criminal.)
- Stage Four: *Law and order.* Astrid should not steal the medicine because the law prohibits stealing, making it illegal. (Or: Astrid should steal the drug for her husband but also take the prescribed punishment for the crime.)

- Stage Five: *Social contract.* Astrid should steal the medicine because everyone has a right to choose life, regardless of the law. (Or: Astrid should not steal the medicine because the scientist has a right to fair compensation, and her rights are as important as the dying man's.)
- Stage Six: *Universal human ethics.* Astrid should steal the medicine, because saving a human life is a more fundamental value than the property rights of another person. (Or: Astrid should not steal the medicine, because others may need the medicine just as badly and their lives are equally significant.)

Although our everyday problems may not be this dramatic, any situation can be deconstructed using this list. An oncologist friend was in an Astrid-esque dilemma recently. A favorite patient of his had slipped into a coma. My friend had been taking care of this woman for several years. She brought him cookies on the days she came in for treatment. Her tumor had been advanced and inoperable long before she became comatose. My friend advised the family to terminate life support. The woman's children threatened to sue him for malpractice if he knowingly allowed their mother to die. He had no choice but to let this sweet lady linger in the hospital for months, suspended in a purgatorial half life of beeping machines and invasive hardware.

There's a difference between allowing something bad to happen and actively making it happen yourself. People ascribe guilt according to intent. We distinguish between doing (or bringing about) and merely allowing. Intention matters because harm is often foreshadowed by intent. "Some forms of merely risking harm to another must be prohibited as well as actually causing harm," philosopher Shelly Kagan tells us. We're biased toward judging actions viewed as intentional more harshly than omissions. This is why most Americans perceive active euthanasia as worse than passive euthanasia.

Most countries allow for passive euthanasia (life support terminated) but block the active kind (when drugs are administered to hasten death). Though the intent and result are the same in both cases, the law requires a medical distinction. It's no surprise to learn that triage doctors in the military find these technical distinctions ridiculous. When you're taking care of mutilated soldiers on the battlefield, legal parsings become so much language. Passive euthanasia is worse, military doctors believe, because the patient suffers longer.

Game Theory

W E'RE FIERCELY COMPETITIVE ANIMALS, passionate about winning and losing. We compete for power, money, status, sex, even virtue: Put two human beings together in a room and sooner or later we'll think up a contest to figure out who's on top. *Homo economicus* (the rational, self-interested actor able to make judgments toward subjectively defined ends) is biologically adapted to carry out a variety of game theory strategies. When these promote individual gain at the expense of the group, we typically consider them bad. If the disparity is extreme enough, we call them evil. Most of us are semi-fair cooperators, though. As tool use and language were watersheds in our evolution, cooperation moved us forward by making it possible for individuals to trust and cohabitate with non-kin. We have done so through the use of non–zero sum games, strategies for win-win outcomes. Over the course of evolution, less-skilled gamers died sooner, on average, and left fewer children. We're descendants of superior cooperators.

But we're also greedy, selfish, and hungry for power. We're easily corrupted by big payoffs—just watch an episode of *Survivor*. The backstabbing, lying, alliance switching, and mudslinging are justi-fied by otherwise decent contestants because there's a million bucks on the table. Most of us wouldn't dream of treating friends the way we treat opponents competing for a coveted prize. But there are healthy and unhealthy ways to compete. Sports are a good example: Even when we lose, we win. Our game is bumped up by competing with our betters. Competition for business improves product and selling strategy. In sexual competition, the mating dance sharpens beneficial characteristics, confidence, sensitivity, and prowess. Altru-ists compete for the greenest technologies. Once-resistant polluters (including General Electric, Monsanto, and DuPont) are tripping over themselves to be politically correct and get on the planet's green side.

Competition becomes destructive only when it opposes the desire for mutual survival, benefiting one individual or group by damaging or eliminating another. When we behave in a winner-take-all way, fear is invoked and a strike-first mentality allows for all sorts of abuses of conscience. On the other hand, cooperative com-petition in which everyone wins—at least, no one walks away with nothing—promotes mutual survival and group fitness. When we compete together against environmental disaster, of course, the best of humanity comes to the fore. We are reminded in such times, as we saw after Hurricane Katrina, that there's only one team in the human race.

Sometimes this herd instinct is deliberate; most of the time it operates beyond intentionality, as if the race itself had a larger "mind" overseeing the welfare of populations. Adam Smith attrib-uted metacooperation to what he called the "invisible hand." According to the invisible hand theory, individuals pursuing their own self-interest in a free market tend to promote the good of the community as well. Maximizing profits for ourselves, we tend to increase the profits to our society as a whole. Obviously, this isn't a

foolproof system; millions of citizens cheat on their taxes and most of us will do everything possible to hoard what we earn rather than share it with the government. The invisible hand giveth and taketh away mostly of its own accord, not because of our personal virtues. "In the same way that humans enjoy sex because it feels good, and only secondarily because sex makes children that benefit population growth, mutual aid originates most often in the desire to please or improve ourselves," scholar Diane Ravitch tells us. She quotes Adam Smith's remark from *The Wealth of Nations* on the unintended social benefits of selfish motivations: "Every individual necessarily labours to render the annual revenue of the society as great as he can. He generally, indeed, neither intends to promote the public interest, nor knows how much he is promoting it . . . It is not from the benevolence of the butcher . . . that we expect our dinner, but from [his] regard to [his] own self-interest."

When people are willing to win at any cost, ethical behavior is sacrificed in proportion to desperation. Hypercompetitive, egomaniacal types have a way of losing all sense of proportion. They're individuals for whom winning isn't everything—it's the only thing. In her pioneering work on human neurosis, psychologist Karen Horney described aggressive personality types who engage in unhealthy competitiveness as "moving against people." To maintain their own self-worth, such people have a compulsive need to compete even when it's not necessary, and if they don't win, God help the people around them. After Passover dinner every year, the kids in my family were enlisted in a dreaded, dangerous Ping-Pong match with my hypercompetitive Uncle Marty. An otherwise good-natured, generous man, Uncle Marty became a stomping, screaming, whining child when a Ping-Pong paddle was in his hand. The transformation was frightening. I used to forfeit our matches as quickly as possible— a victory wasn't worth the grief! He once stormed out of the house before the Afikomen, the matzoh-hiding ritual, when my cousin

Ronnie dared to beat him. It was funny but also kind of sad. Ronnie was only twelve years old.

There's a degree of tension between cooperation and competition in all of us. Our ethics are regularly tested by how we choose to play the game. Think of the prisoner's dilemma. Let me offer a bit of a variation on this classic game theory plum. George and Laura have been arrested by the police. George and Laura are friends but not *close* friends. They hooked up at a barbecue in San Diego, maybe, and had a little too much sangria before George—who wanted to sleep with Laura—agreed to drive across the border into Tijuana and smuggle Laura's Mexican aunt into the country to see her grandchildren. George and Laura are now being interrogated in different rooms by border police because the hidden Mexican aunt had a coughing fit while the immigration guys were checking the rig.

It could happen to anybody.

The cops have separated George and Laura, hoping that they will rat each other out. At issue, let's say, is whether or not they knew the aunt was stashed in the RV's crawl space. It's the difference between premeditated smuggling of an illegal alien and being the hapless victim of a very limber Mexican grandma with the ability to fold herself in two. George and Laura know the score, more or less. They realize that although lying is not morally correct, neither is it fair for them to go to jail for trying to do a good deed and not hurting anyone, technically. George and Laura meant no harm. Lacking sufficient evidence for a conviction, the border cops offer them the same plea deal. If one betrays the other (but the betrayed party remains silent), the "defector" goes free and the silent accomplice receives the full ten-year sentence. If both George and Laura remain loyal (and silent), each is sentenced to only six months in jail for a minor charge. But if they betray each other, each receives a five-year sentence. Each party is assured that the other half will not know about the betrayal before the end of the investigation.

What should George and Laura do?

The prisoner's dilemma is an exercise designed to expose the limitations of loyalty, as well as the statistical likelihood of cooperation, between individuals who don't want to stay in jail. If we assume that each player prefers shorter sentences to longer ones, that neither benefits from lowering the other player's sentence, and that there are no reputation effects from a player's decision, then the prisoner's dilemma forms a non–zero-sum game. Game theory dictates that the rational choice would lead both George and Laura to defect, even though each player's individual reward would be greater if they both played cooperatively.

In the classic form of this game, defection trumps cooperation. The prisoner's dilemma becomes more interesting, however, when the game is played repeatedly and prisoners have an opportunity to punish each other for previous noncooperative play. This more closely resembles the real world, where actions are often knowable through gossip and reputation is at stake. In such cases, the incentive to defect can be overcome by the threat of punishment or social rejection. When such experiments are repeated over a long period of time, with many players, greedy strategies do, indeed, tend to do poorly, while altruistic strategies do better in the long run. This is not to whitewash our selfishness; we cooperate out of self-interest, mainly, though we acknowledge noncooperation to be a lose-lose, and why gyp others if we don't have to? But when others *stop* reciprocating, we waste no time in doing the same; this is the meaning of tit for tat. Retaliation may begin when generosity ceases. Or we may choose a higher road.

Altruism

ALTRUISTIC ACTS ARE PERFORMED, or not, depending on a precise cost-benefit analysis called Hamilton's Rule. For us to be altruistic, this theorem goes, the cost (c) to the altruist must be less than the benefit (b) to the recipient multiplied by the coefficient of relatedness (r). This means that the more closely related two organisms are, the more the incidence of altruism will increase. It should come as no surprise to learn that people who perform altruistic acts *without* an emotional basis—guilt, generosity, gratitude, or duty—may be less reliable in the future. Organisms that benefit from the altruistic act, and respond on behalf of their own fitness, increase their own chances of survival and reproduction. Once again, this cycle tends to radiate outward from the kin group with decreasing frequency and diminished benefit to the altruist.

But Hamilton's Rule isn't written in stone. Altruism is prized so highly in moral life because it is both costly and freely given. By its nature, altruism reaches; like love, it extends beyond the self at personal expense. And like art, as well as love, altruism offers dividends of satisfaction that frequently transcend expectation. I like what Reinhold Niebuhr, the religious writer, says about this. "Those agents who most effectively achieve the greatest amount of good possible in a situation," he writes, "may be the ones who do more than simply identify with others," but who also "believe in the spontaneous movements of sacrificial love, in their radical and utopian proponents." How beautiful is that? Such giving souls "may overcome obstacles that seem hopeless to more cautious and 'realistic' spirits, because nothing but such madness will do battle with malignant power and spiritual wickedness."

Altruists tend to fall into two camps: reformers and helpers. Each of these altruistic types has a distinctive personality and helping style. Reformers are oriented to correcting social injustice. They tend to show a zest for combat and adventure, and are much more likely to express anger or contempt in their altruistic campaigns. Helpers, on the other hand, are motivated by a desire to alleviate suffering. They tend to be more nurturing, and to identify with the distress of the people they are helping. Helpers are less likely than reformers to exhibit anger.

Where do you fall between these two camps? Are you more moved by the thought of helping or reforming in the world? (I'm more of a helper myself.) In his study of Gentiles who rescued Jews during World War II, Samuel Oliner, a Holocaust survivor, found commonalities among those who had developed in the altruistic direction. Rescuers were apt to describe their early family relationships, particularly with their mothers, as "intimate" far more frequently than nonrescuers. Rescuers also felt significantly closer to their fathers. Rescuers had learned about the satisfactions that derive from personal bonds with others from this early intimacy. The relationship to our parents forms our first layer—ground zero—in how we approach our later lives, as we know.

What distinguishes rescuers from nonrescuers is their tendency to be moved by pain. Empathy for pain does not necessarily result in a helping response, however. Instead of helping, one may cop out, Samuel and Pearl Oliner write, "by physically removing oneself from the problem, denying it, devaluing the victim, or contenting oneself with some slight gesture." Just as rescuers' greater proclivity toward attachment to others emerged early in life, so did their inclusive orientation—their feelings of connection to diverse people and groups. More frequently than non-rescuers, rescuers reported youthful tendencies to feel similar to a wider and more diverse range of people.

Rescuers' stronger sense of personal efficacy, the Oliners found—their feeling that they could affect events and were responsible for doing do—was reflected in their scores on J. B. Rotter's Internal/External Locus of Control Scale (to which you'll find a link at the end of this book). Locus of control refers to the extent to which individuals believe that they can control events that affect them. Do we operate from an internal power source, or do we see ourselves as hapless victims of circumstance? Parents whose disciplinary techniques are benevolent, particularly those who rely on reasoning, are more likely to have kind and generous internal-locus kids, who behave helpfully and with respect toward others. According to the Oliners, "We learn by early inductive reasoning the consequences of our actions on others, focusing on their feelings, thoughts, and welfare." This is how children learn cognitive empathy.

When parents encourage generosity, and communicate the obligation to help others in a spirit of magnanimity without concern for external rewards or reciprocity, they open pathways for altruism in their children. Being expected to care for others while simultaneously being cared for, children learn to become "extensive." They learn self-reliance as well as compassion. Extensive people are more likely to evaluate themselves positively, further reinforcing the tendency to be helpful toward others. As they continue throughout their lives to help others, they are also more likely to transmit such values to their own children.

At the opposite end of the generosity spectrum are "constricted" people. Insecure and suspicious, constricted people are wary of neighbors and peers. They expect others to take advantage of them and tend toward disproportionate self-protection. With a tendency toward misanthropy, they have a pessimistic view of other people, believing them to lack integrity, and so, instead of risking attachments, constricted individuals like to go it alone (even in coupled relationships). They're so aware of their own vulnerabilities that they cannot trust others, or expose themselves to a world they find threatening. Instead, constricted types tend to blame others for their lack of satisfaction and feel paradoxically anxious about losing the handful of social contacts they have.

In other words, anxiety affects our ability to give. Our innate impulse to help can become muddled, suppressed, or overridden when we feel insecurely attached. Where secure people are likely to be the most compassionate, constricted people tend to be swallowed up by their own distressing reactions and unable to rouse themselves to calls for help. While insecure people may feel others' pain, those feelings can intensify into "empathic distress," a level of anxiety so strong that they become overwhelmed. They are vulnerable to compassion fatigue as well, and tend to get buried under personal anguish when forced to witness suffering. Empathic distress can be overcome, however. In one study, anxious subjects were told to think about people in their own lives who cared about them. Afterward, they were strikingly able to overcome their own resistance to helping, having enhanced their own feelings of security.

The thought flows into the deed. Flow is a useful metaphor when thinking about altruism, and about moral behavior generally. While we're separate beings, we are also inextricably bound to those around us. Indeed, we *are* the world, as any physicist will tell you. All of us are bound in what Buddhists call Indra's Net: the vast web-work of interdependent entities comprising Creation, strung on the tension of cause and effect. Every single action we make causes a reaction in our immediate vicinity on this rippling net. Mihaly Csikszentmihalyi, a psychologist at the University of Chicago, is the father of "flow." Flow experiences, he explains, are those moments of optimal psychological functioning, when we're so engrossed in what we are doing that we seem to move outside (or beyond) ourselves, losing consciousness of self. When self-interest falls away for a moment and we're simply *doing* whatever it is that's at hand, we are "flowing" in our lives. Worries about material gain, personal achievement, security, and so on are absorbed in present-moment attention. Spacey as this may sound, we're actually more awake, alert, and activated during flow moments than we are in the rest of our lives, Csikszentmihalyi explains, but so focused on what we are doing that mundane concerns that would otherwise distract us don't affect us at all. This is useful information for constricted people. "The hero and the saint, to the extent that they dedicate the totality of their psychic energy into an all-encompassing goal that prescribes a coherent pattern of behavior to follow until death, turn their lives into unified flow experiences," he writes. "Whatever we do must be unified around an abiding concern for good." Sometimes we can even transcend selfish habits of tit for tat, cost-benefit analysis, reputation management, and other preoccupations concerned with getting ahead and staying there. We are made, after all, to live in packs.

Man Is Wolf to Man

[LOYALTY]

Part Three

One of the dominant elements [in all men's lives] is the desire to be inside the local Ring and the terror of being left outside . . . Of all the passions the passion for the Inner Ring is the most skillful in making a man who is not yet a very bad man do very bad things.

—C. S. LEWIS

Loyalty

A FEW YEARS BACK, I was cramped into a Fifth Avenue bus, inching its way through bumper-to-bumper traffic, when a hoopla erupted on the street outside. At first, I couldn't see what had happened; then a purse snatcher appeared with a stolen handbag, tearing down the sidewalk away from a group of Good Samaritans who happened to have witnessed the theft. In a New York minute, this posse of anonymous strangers had chased down the creep—automatically—thrown him to the ground, and pinned him there till the plainclothes cops arrived with handcuffs and led him to a squad car. The grateful lady was reunited with her handbag. The crowd left, the bus moseyed on, and another dishonest creep bit the dust.

But how had this happened so quickly? How had a SWAT team of random strangers formed at a particular moment to avenge a woman they didn't know? With no hope of reward? Thomas Hobbes, the pessimistic seventeenth-century philosopher who popularized the phrase *Homo homini lupus*—man is wolf to man—and used this canine comparison to emphasize how selfish and savage people can be, downplayed the upside of pack life: it makes us more effective when working together for the common good. To help ensure one another's survival, we pack into groups, care for each other, hunt together, and come together to retrieve stolen accessories. Distress prompts solidarity. Zoologists call this "spontaneous emergent organization," in which a large number of prey animals attack a larger predator, in self-defense or aggression. Under attack, dolphins form a "magic envelope" to protect the threatened individual. When sharks or killer whales approach, the envelope tightens in a flash, as a way of confusing the predators with a coordinated response faster than their eyes can follow, similarly to how this crowd on Fifth Avenue automatically packed together to trap this crook.

Humans thrive on pack behavior. We're designed to form groups that oppose other groups—we like to belong and we like to draw boundaries. We ground identity in citizenship to a larger body—family, church, nation, or race—and will fight for our home turf's survival, sometimes to the death. "Man defending his honor and the welfare of his ethnic group is man defending himself," after all, as sociologist Milton Gordon tells us. Tribal psychology is so deeply pleasurable to the brain, psychologists assure us, that few of us can resist it even if we try. Since moral life requires solidarity, no one is more loathed than a traitor. Traitors cannot be countenanced in a pack. While murder is considered the most serious crime today, treason was an even worse offense in the past. According to English law, high treason was punishable by being hanged, drawn, and quartered if you were a man, or being burned at the stake if you were a woman. The near-enemy of loyalty is xenophobia. Fear of outsiders, extreme nationalism, blind obedience, and mechanical conformity are the dangers of excessive loyalty. Xenophobia blinds individuals to the faults of their own group (remember the bumper stickers that read AMERICA LOVE IT OR LEAVE IT) and can easily prompt mob responses to perceived outside threats.

Loyalty is a two-sided moral emotion. In a world increasingly interconnected by technology and cultural osmosis, where the notion of "global community" is bandied about if not strictly obeyed, loyalty in an us-versus-them sense is quickly becoming obsolete. Tribal tendencies are largely outdated and augur a violent future. At least one hundred million people have been murdered in the past century due to some version of in-group loyalty, but this ethic of loyalty threatens to keep us stuck in a wanton, bloody past. Playing Eleanor of Aquitaine in the film *Lion in Winter*, Katharine Hepburn summed it up nicely, surveying the carnage around her castle. "It's 1183 and we're still barbarians," Hepburn's cynical queen lamented. She was wearing a medieval tiara when she said it but our situation hasn't changed all that much. Actually, it's gotten worse.

Loyalty—as a source of aggression—appears to be linked to feelings of powerlessness, psychologists tell us. The more powerless people feel in their lives, the more likely they are to form angry mobs. The lower the standard of living, the more likely individuals are to jump on board with isolationist policies that oppress outsiders (or those less fortunate than they are). The more empowered people feel, on the other hand, the more satisfied with their lot in life, the less defensive and threatened they tend to be. This suggests that we can shrink or stretch our "circle of care" depending on our personal sense of well-being (as we've seen with extensive versus constricted types of people). This expansion of loyalty can occur without losing personal identity or the traditions, customs, and creeds we cherish. Group uniqueness is not the problem—it's the either-or part that screws us up. When tribal love supersedes love of species, humankind becomes a doomed pack.

But is it really possible to be loyal to the family of man first, our individual pack second? That is the ethical koan of modern life. Similar to those deliberately unanswerable teaching questions posed by Zen masters to their students to help them think outside the box, we ask ourselves if it is possible to crack the too-low ceiling of kin selection, extend the walls of group selection, and move as a species toward a time when we view ourselves as wolf-cells inside a larger wolf-body, *without* sacrificing smaller-group loyalty. In our personal cells, our groups, our families, we recognize the need to cohere and trust; it remains true that charity begins at home. We're obliged by nature to stick with our people, to help those closest to us before turning attention to others. But this does not preclude a larger vision. The ethical tenet of filial piety, put forth by Confucius and still revered in Chinese culture, does not preclude extending our empathic boundaries. Filial piety means being good to one's parents, having fraternity with relations, and protecting one's good name. But it also means, increasingly, being loyal to the family of man.

Filial piety and clan loyalty tend to increase in proportion to outside threats. Families pack together to protect themselves, and clans benefit from strength found in numbers. My best friend comes from a clan of Russian immigrants straight out of the book *Tough Jews,* a Semitic bunch of generous borderline mobsters. The Levithans are a stand-apart bunch, unusually devoted to their family and proud of one another. In America, members of the tall, blue-eyed clan were able to pass as Gentiles while remaining privately true to their Jewish roots; they would not be oppressed by anti-Semitism in the new country as they had been in Russia. Their Aryan appearance helped them to procure jobs that other Jews couldn't get. As Robert Levithan tells me, "My family were capitalists when it came to the outside world, socialists when it came to each other. If one person had, then nobody did without." With relatives who'd perished in the pogroms, their cardinal rule was: stick together. "My family was intensely loyal to each other," says Robert. "It made for a lot of secret keeping."

"Why secret keeping?"

"My grandmother Fanny used to say that the only people you

can trust is each other," Robert says, imitating her with a perfect New England accent and wag of his finger. Outsiders might turn on you. That's why these assimilated Jews camouflaged themselves in a Christian country. "Everything was about *passing*. Nobody could have an accent because it would blunt the family's competitive edge. Presentation in the world was *everything*."

"And the secrets?"

"They kept secrets so as not to weaken the clan," he explains. "And the world seemed safer because we were part of this big family group."

Loyalty meant unconditional forgiveness. "I always knew that no matter what happened, my family would always accept me," says Robert with a chuckle. "Since people weren't thrown out of the family for being felons, liars, and cheats, there wasn't much danger of me not being accepted! It was a safe feeling, but the secret keeping made me uneasy. This kind of a model didn't really embrace people outside the family." The flip side of solidarity is alienation and rigidly defined (and defended) group boundaries.

Us Versus Them

GROUP SELF-FAVORITISM REMAINS our greatest ethical albatross. "Human beings are consistent in their codes of honor but endlessly fickle with reference to whom the codes apply," E. O. Wilson points out. "The genius of human sociality is in fact the ease with which alliances are formed, broken, and reconstituted, always with emotional appeals to rules believed to be absolute." If all men deserve equal justice for no other reason than that they are men, however, exclusive loyalty doesn't work.

The drive to form in-groups is always shadowed by the creation of out-groups, whose members are automatically less deserving of everything for no other reason than that they're not us. The price of loyalty to our own group is always aversion toward another. We have an irresistible urge to dichotomize human beings into opposing categories. We seem to be comfortable only when the remainder of humanity may be labeled as *them*. When there's a history of enmity between groups, we're likely to fall prey to what Sigmund Freud called "the narcissism of minor differences." This is the sort of antipathy that haunts closely related tribes, such as the Greeks and

Turks, the Tutsi and Hutu, and the Indians and the Pakistanis. This group-splitting causes violence; it also makes for some very dark humor. Indeed, there is only one type of universal human joke—what we generally call a Polish joke. According to Lance Morrow, "The Flemish have Walloon jokes, the English tell Irish jokes, the Hutu have Tutsi jokes and the people of Tokyo have jokes about the people of Osaka." Once, on a train from Brussels to Paris, a French-man regaled me for hours about his countrymen's superiority to the Belgians, beginning with waffles ("*affreux!*" he scoffed, *awful*) and ending with an aesthetic apotheosis of the House of Dior. His minor-difference narcissism was ridiculous but he could not have cared less.

To understand how things like racism take place in the first place, though, we need to understand how stereotyping helped us survive in the past, and why we no longer need it. Stereotyping is an evolutionary mechanism that provides visual shorthand for threat-ened creatures avoiding enemies in a brutal world. From an early age, our minds become seduced by the opportunity to form cate-gories, turning the messiness of the world into an orderly zone of recognizable types and races. Our preconceived stereotyping ideas attribute certain general characteristics to all the members of a class or set. These stereotypes then fix themselves in the psyche by corre-lating variables that are only loosely associated, if at all. This is a cor-ruption of a normal cognitive function: categorization. (In fact, the word "stereotype" derives from the Greek for "solid" and "impres-sion.") We carve out solid-seeming, fixed impressions of types or groups and use these generalizations to make snap judgments. Such categories help us to order our world and provide us with quick information: By assuming that the next entity they encountered in a given category had the same main features as the last, our ancestors saved time and bloodshed. Though inaccurate, stereotyping is highly efficient in this sense. Unfortunately, after we've organized everyone into tidy categories, we have every reason to avoid processing new or unexpected information that suggests people *don't* fit their stereotype. Locking people into place by typing them also helps us feel good about ourselves. Designating one's own group as the standard or "normal" group, and assigning others to groups considered inferior or abnormal, protects us from anxiety and boosts our feelings of self-worth. The House of Dior wasn't built in *Belgium.*

Stereotypes and their wicked spawn, prejudice, tend to appear early in psychological life, before the beliefs that are used to justify them make their appearance. This is why prejudice is morally dumbfounding; reaching inward for the reason that we hate (fill in the blank), we come up with nothing but rationalizations. Once a negative bias is formed in us, our emotional lenses are forever clouded unless we wipe off the *shmutz* ourselves. Prejudice is also self-perpetuating: scanning our environs, our minds seize on whatever they can to confirm our biases and disregard evidence to the contrary. Like hypotheses trying to prove themselves, stereotypes tend to be self-fulfilling and derogatory. For early man, it may have been better to be safe than sorry, but this moral hardware is very crude, indeed; it's frequently stupid and stubbornly wrong. My slightly paranoid spinster neighbor yelps every time I—a tall, dark-skinned man—step into the elevator behind her wearing a ski cap. Flooded by fight-flight limbic emotions, her cortex is hijacked by phobic stereotyping that turns me into a mugger, though we've lived next door to each other for ten years. When reason is incapacitated, we're unable to ask ourselves corrective questions. Does this person *really* seem dangerous? Do these foreigners *really* have the bad traits I ascribe to them? Is there any reason to think that this ski cap is worn by a dangerous person? Are Belgian people really tackier than the French? Because stereotypes and prejudices lie tucked away in the unconscious recesses of the mind, however, they're hard to locate and dismantle.

To make matters worse, stereotypes become bound to fixed emotional patterns in us that privilege the in-group types over outsiders. Nature has empowered us with a "hostile imagination" for the same reason that we're born with a negativity bias. "Otherness" alienates automatically. "Should one of *them* [italics mine] presume to speak to one of us, the voice would not be heard as fully or openly as would that of one of us—if at all," Daniel Goleman explains. "The gulf that divides us from them builds with the silencing of empathy." In this silence, I-You becomes I-It, and a bloody line is drawn in the sand. Philosopher Martin Buber put it this way: "With the words us-them, the world is divided into two: the children of light and the children of darkness, the sheep and the goats, the elect and the damned." Spiritual teacher Eckhart Tolle described this to me in different terms. "When we label other people, they become concepts," Tolle explained. "When people become concepts, it becomes possible to treat them in any way that we like. This is how such atrocities are possible between human beings. It is the label, the concept, that is the cause."

The habit of labeling others, which most of us do a lot of the time ("foreigner," "poor," "rich," "conservative," "faggot," "Commie," "Arab," "slut"), helps us turn *them* into objects unworthy of full consideration. Individuals in categories become ciphers. Objectified and dehumanized, they cease to rouse our fellow feeling. This is how ethnic cleansing can happen. Conquerors and dictators have long known that the best way to get people to think as a group is to identify an enemy and charge that "they" threaten "us." It seems ironic that morality itself emerged from precisely the same aggressive impulse; the threat of war forced in-group solidarity to increase to the point that out-group hostility could be mastered. "Humankind's noblest achievement—morality—has evolutionary ties to our basest behavior," writes de Waal. "The sense of community required by the former was provided by the latter."

The need to be accepted, respected, and liked—to "fit in" as normal and appropriate—is so powerful that we're primed to conform to the most outlandish behaviors (and the cruelest and most heartless as well, like blowing ourselves up for Allah). More than a decade before 9/11, Richard Dawkins warned presciently in *The Selfish Gene* that "a species or a population within a species whose individual members are prepared to sacrifice themselves for the welfare of the group, may be less likely to go extinct than a rival group whose individual members place their own selfish interests first." This is precisely how terror operates and why, at the end of the day, Americans know that the religious martyrs have the advantage. Autocratic and hate-mongering as some media pundits may be, you won't find Rush Limbaugh strapping a bomb to his chest and praying for virgins in paradise. It is odd to learn that suicide bombers exist elsewhere in the animal kingdom; there is a species of Malaysian ant whose members of the soldier caste store a sticky substance just under their exoskeletons and explode their bodies in the midst of battle, like insect-sized Islamofascists. They come, they conquer, they blow themselves up.

The good news about us versus them is that stereotyping can be reversed. A recent study of prejudice revealed that mutual trust can catch on and spread between different racial groups just as quickly as suspicion. Through something known as the "extended-contact effect," which travels like a benign virus through opposing groups, "conscious as well as unconscious bias between people of different races can change in a matter of hours," according to psychology researchers at the University of Massachusetts. Peaceful exposure to "the other" seems to be key. Programs like the Oseh Shalom-Sanea al-Salam Palestinian-Jewish Family Peacemakers Camp, where Jewish and Arab youth have the opportunity to spend time together in a natural setting, offer clues for how larger-scale initiatives might be devised to break down the us-versus-them blockade. By stepping beyond the insider threshold, we pierce the narcissist illusion conjured by groups for their own benefit.

Group Narcissism

MY FAVORITE DESCRIPTION OF NARCISSISM comes from Erich Fromm. In *The Anatomy of Human Destructiveness*, Fromm's paean to emotional demonry, the great psychologist describes this delusional state as one "in which only the [narcissist] himself, *his* body, *his* needs, *his* feelings, *his* thoughts, *his* property, everything and everybody pertaining to *him* are experienced as fully real, while everybody and everything [else] . . . is [perceived only] intellectually." Like the mythic youth trapped by his own reflection, narcissists view the world around them as if through a self-mirroring glass that reduces other people to mere functionaries, sidekicks in the narcissist's grandiose dream.

Group narcissism occurs when this self-cherishing is projected onto our collective identity. Group narcissism, with its obvious reliance on consensus reality, is our compensation for not feeling especially worthy ourselves, psychologists tell us. If my group is wonderful, the logic goes, then I become wonderful simply by belonging to it. It's hard to go around shouting "I'm the greatest!" but you can absolutely scream "America's the greatest country on earth!" from the rooftops and be viewed as patriotic, not crazy.

Narcissistic group loyalty allows us to express egotistical supremacy without restrictions, promoting ourselves as model citizens in the process. As Fromm observed, "An individual, unless he is mentally very sick, may have at least some doubts about his personal narcissistic image. The member of the group has none, since his narcissism is shared by the majority." Also, if our in-group is never wrong, then it's *they* who have the shortcomings. We can project our defects onto out-group members and hide inside the myth of our own perfection. The enemy is bad but I'm all good. I mean, *we're* all good, which is almost the same, right?

Even if you're miserable, or lowly, you can still be a (fill in the blank). In fact, like mob behavior, the degree of group narcissism has been shown to be commensurate with lack of real satisfaction in life. The poorer the in-group, the more it uses group narcissism as a form of compensation. Misery loves company, which is why poor people are so easily manipulated. But the dividing line needn't be financial; there are plenty of unhappy middle-class people who band in narcissistic packs, as the real housewives of Washington, D.C. prove every week on trash TV. With the narcissistic group packaging complete, we're free to exercise our repressed aggression.

Members of narcissistic groups tend to overreact to criticism from outsiders. Think for a moment of Kim Jong Il, the Garbo-esque leader of North Korea, swanning in his hairdo and fake soldier's getup, taking world opinion against his national policies so *deeply* personally. The country appears to be a stand-in for Kim's own wounded ego. Narcissistic groups (and their leaders) tend to be isolationist at heart, protecting the myth of their own omnipotence behind mirrors gilded with propaganda. In Maoist China, "the Chinese knew the narcissistic joy of loving themselves through [Mao]," notes French philosopher Alain Peyrifitte, "and it [was] only natural he should have loved himself through them." In our own country's history, group narcissism has conjured a whole slew of make-believe enemies (Commies and "anti-Americans," to name two), justifying political, religious, and personal witch hunts over perceived breaches of loyalty. So-called traitors have their characters assassinated by the self-defensive mob. Remember what happened to Natalie Maines, the lead singer of the Dixie Chicks? Maines had gone public with her antiwar beliefs following the American invasion of Iraq—adding how ashamed she was that then-president Bush hailed from her home state of Texas—only to be roasted to a crisp on the barbecue of right-wing disdain. The Dixie Chicks saw their albums burned in public protest and their concert attendance cut in half. By speaking out against war while our troops were fighting overseas, Maines—like so many before her—was tarred with a traitor's brush and branded a moral pariah.

Resistance to group pressure comes at a higher neurological cost than conformity, the fMRI machine tells us. In an experiment measuring group pressure, it was found that subjects challenged to agree with incorrect information caved in to the majority, agreeing with their wrong answers, a startling 41 percent of the time. Autonomy comes at a psychic cost. "We like to think that seeing is believing, but the study's findings show that seeing is believing what the group tells you to believe," concluded the lead author of this work, Gregory Berns. Ask yourself about your own group narcissism(s). Do you personally censor yourself on account of fidelity to some exclusive group? Do you participate in activities you don't believe in, or which have no meaning for you, so that the group will accept you? What parts of yourself do you lop off, or hide, or file in the drawer marked "inconvenient truths" in order not to be called a traitor? Do you oppress others when you are feeling oppressed, or use group narcissism to puff yourself up and blind yourself to personal (or communal) failings?

Israeli psychologist Sam Vaknin has attempted to connect the dots between group narcissism—which he terms mass psychopathology—and global violence. Groups become dangerous, Vaknin believes, when they form a "condensate," the term used by physicists to describe a material in which all the atoms are vibrating at the same frequency. Normally, Vaknin writes, "group behavior resembles diffuse light." But when a population has been traumatized, as many Israeli Jews have been, he believes that the group may form a "malignant laser" aimed at its oppressors (or perceived oppressors). "The group becomes abusive to others, exploitative, detached from reality, bathed in grandiose fantasies, xenophobic, lacking empathy, prone to uncontrolled rages, over-sensitive, convinced of its superiority and entitlement," Vaknin contends. Force and coercion may be used to disabuse such narcissistic groups of their delusions, but these are likely to cement a group's vanity and sense of victimization, and justify its adversarial ethos.

Narcissistic groups feed their own power hunger using the gruel of victimhood. Indeed, Vaknin has claimed that being an Israeli provided him with "privileged insight into [the] fascinating transformation from tortured slave to vengeful master." Whether or not we agree with his anti-Zionist sentiments—personally, I find them exaggerated and tinged with narcissistic self-loathing—Vaknin's point is an important one. Whether we use the example of the Israelis, or the Hutu, or those loyal to Osama bin Laden, it cannot be denied that oppressed groups have a tendency to fuel their own narcissistic defenses, and engender in-group loyalty, by vilifying their purported oppressors. The relationship between humiliation (perceived or real) and narcissistic aggression is volatile and dangerous. According to Vaknin, this anger is spawned by a "gap between reality and [the group's] grandiose fantasies, between actual inferiority and a delusional sense of superiority (and cosmic mission)."

In *Civilization and Its Discontents,* where Freud introduced "the narcissism of minor differences," he blamed this futile, perpetual victim-perp cycle on our need for a sense of supremacy. It is "not easy for man to give up the satisfaction of this inclination to aggression," Freud warned. "It is always possible to bind together a considerable number of people in love, so long as there are other people left over to receive the manifestations of their aggressiveness." Animosity toward the other increases in-group loyalty whether stereotyped outsiders actually pose a threat or not. Without enemies, how can we defend our honor? Without feeling victimized, how can we prevail? Without believing that our group is the best one, how can we feel worthy in a world teeming with competition? The loftier our group narcissism, the more fanatical we can be. No group has ever been more blindly narcissistic than the German SS, obsessed with creating a purified world in their own ultra white image. On October 3, 1943, at the height of the Nazis' mechanized annihilation—the "peak of production," in their twisted parlance—Heinrich Himmler, then head of the German police, wrote out a mission statement to the SS:

> We must be honest, decent, loyal, and comradely to members of our own blood, and to nobody else. What happens to the Russians, what happens to the Czechs, is a matter of total indifference to me . . . *It is a crime against our hard won blood to worry about them and to give them ideals that will make it still harder for our sons and grandsons to cope with them* [italics mine]. Our concern, our duty, is to our own people and our blood . . . Toward anything else we can be indifferent . . . I wish the SS to take this attitude in confronting the problem of all alien, non-Germanic peoples, especially the Russians. All else is just soap bubbles.

Such stupendous narcissism leaves a moral person speechless.

Memes

GROUP ANIMOSITY AND STEREOTYPING perpetuate themselves through the spread of memes. Memes are ideas that replicate virally in populations. Because they are self-transcendent, memes also transcend time. Indeed, "the meme complexes of Socrates, Leonardo, Copernicus and Marconi are still going strong today," according to Richard Dawkins. First introduced in *The Selfish Gene,* memes (from the Greek for "something imitated") range from beliefs to melodies, catchphrases, fashions, fads, and ideologies that are spread through the behaviors that they generate. While genes are the basis for *organic* evolution, memes form the units of *cultural* evolution. These hard-to-measure fragments of information coalesce in us to constitute our communal estimations of good and evil. Memes range from innocuous slogans ("blondes have more fun") to hate speech ("Jews killed Jesus") to calls for benevolence ("save the planet by living 'green'"). The Internet has ramped up memetic imitation by a factor of quadrillions, as networks like Twitter and YouTube spread images and ideas instantaneously around the clock and around the globe.

In his book *Cultural Software,* Jack Balkin tells us that memetic processes explain many of the most familiar features of ideological thought, because memes are the info-bytes that help to form personal and group identity. The same structures used to generate ideas about free speech and free markets can also spread bitterness and stereotypes. In Part Five, you'll meet a remorseful ex-capo from South Africa's apartheid movement. Confronting the widow of a black man he ordered to be executed, the former racist is overcome by emotion. "I was raised to think of you as an animal," he tells the widow, shamefully. Racism is a meme passed darkly from branch to branch on a family tree, then throughout a culture's root system, until it seems to be part of the tree itself.

God is the greatest meme of all. Indeed, all religions are meme complexes that spread their beliefs in the form of gospel. Memes for religion are passed from parent to child. Most people will hold the religion taught to them by their parents throughout their life. It's not accidental that most religions feature some enemy or other, since you can't have God without the Devil. In religions such as Christianity, the meme of conversion is especially strong; believers are taught to view conversion as a religious duty as well as an act of altruism. The promise of eternity in heaven to believers, or hell to nonbelievers, provides a strong incentive to accept and retain religious faith. Also, it has been suggested that the crucifixion in Christianity amplifies the meme of sacrifice and indebtedness to a savior, who in turn deserves our loyalty and self-giving.

It is the meme for reciprocity as ratified by the Golden Rule, though, that provides us with the foundation stone for ethical strength. This meme has been echoed by different cultures to the same effect:

- "What thou avoidest suffering thyself seek not to impose on others." [EPICTETUS]

- "Do to every man as thou wouldst have him do to thee; and do not unto another what thou wouldst not have done to thee." [CONFUCIUS]

- "One who, while himself seeking happiness, oppresses with violence other beings who also desire happiness will not attain happiness hereafter." [BUDDHA]

- "Do not seek revenge or bear a grudge against one of your people, but love your neighbor as yourself." [JUDAISM]

- "And as ye would that men should do to you, do ye also to them likewise." [CHRISTIANITY]

- "One should never do that to another which one regards as injurious to one's own self." [HINDUISM]

- "Hurt no one so that no one may hurt you." [ISLAM]

- "Regard your neighbor's gain as your own gain, and your neighbor's loss as your own loss." [TAOISM]

From these seeds, the meme of goodness is spread. "Saying with our actions that no one need fear us is one of the greatest contributions we can give to the world," Joseph Goldstein, a Buddhist teacher, explains. "Our non-harming offers the gift of safety and trust to all those around us. Morality brings us the peace of non-remorse. Through our commitment and practice of non-harming"—in actions of body, speech, and mind—"the suffering of regret, which can be such a powerfully negative force in our lives, does not agitate our minds. When our minds are not agitated, concentration comes more easily. From concentration comes the birth of wisdom."

Sociologists tell us that memes for virtue can elevate populations against the odds. As Colby and Damon note, "When the minority's behavior is perceived as both extreme *and* virtuous by the majority, sooner or later the majority will move in the direction of the admired minority." The democratic meme that individuals can make a difference for the group marked a giant step forward for our species. No longer was it enough to belong to the pack; societies began to insist that individuals try to make a difference for the better. Even in the most vicious societies, there have always been "outstanding personalities who embodied the highest form of human existence," Fromm tells us. Some of them have been spokesmen for humanity, "saviors" without whom man might have lost the vision of his goal. Others have remained unknown. These secret heroes are the ones the Jewish legend refers to as the thirty-six just men in each generation, whose existence guarantees the survival of mankind. These elevational superstars have perpetuated altruistic memes and encouraged their followers to pass them down to the next generations.

Take a moment to consider how your own life is affected by memes of good and evil—ideas you've picked up from your parents, at school, or from Jon Stewart clowning on TV. Consider how many received ideas may have been absorbed, unquestioned, by your mind, and helped to form your personal belief system. Now try doing an experiment with memes. First, locate a belief in your inner landscape that has never quite made sense to you, but which you've held on to nevertheless. We all have bad ideological fits, and if you survey your own psyche carefully, you're sure to find one (where's Waldo?). Now, close your eyes and imagine lifting this idea from its mental groove, and setting it on your mental table. Open your eyes and locate a pen and paper. When's the first time you remember hearing this idea? Write it down. From whom did you hear it, or was this received idea just "in the air"? If you can recall who introduced this idea to you, how did they explain it? Or didn't they bother? Now, if you can, state as clearly as possible why you believe this meme, or belief, to be patently false. Once you've done this, pause for a moment to see how you feel. Is there a slant of light in your mind that wasn't there five minutes ago? If so, you may have displaced a meme.

Memes are socially learned mirrored behaviors, not built-in mirrored behaviors like yawning or smiling. Memes need to have a built-in hook of some kind, some intrinsic means of self-defense and justification. Take the meme of heaven and hell. Regardless of whether they're real or not, just look at the way these memes affect how people view the world. Hellfire and brimstone have haunted us down through the ages based on nothing, perhaps, but legend, then repeated and repeated as true. One generation after another consumes and digests these memes; finally, they seem inseparable from our thinking. In the case of heaven and hell, these memes reinforce one another, endlessly, and assist in one another's survival in the meme pool. They both rely on faith, the most dangerous meme of all, if we believe the anti-God squad (Christopher Hitchens, Sam Harris, Bill Maher, et al.). "The meme for blind faith secures its perpetuation by discouraging rational inquiry," such brights complain. They aren't wrong. Blind faith can justify anything, including killing atheists. "If a man believes in a different god or worships differently, blind faith can decree that he should die, on the cross, at the stake, on the crusader's sword, in a Beirut street, or blown up in Belfast," writes Richard Dawkins.

Memes are also ethically blind, which is why we must examine them closely. It's interesting to learn that social custom tends to trump religious memes, even in puritanical communities. When Mennonite and Amish children were asked, in a 2001 study, whether it would be okay to work on a Sunday if God said so, 100 percent of the subjects said yes. When asked if it would be okay to steal if God said so, over 80 percent said no. "Such findings belong to a compelling body of evidence that moral prescriptions and values [memes] are experienced as 'objective' in the sense that they don't seem to depend on us, or on any authoritative figure," said Larry Nucci, who authored this study.

The more an ideology pretends to give answers to all questions, the more attractive it will be—regardless of its accuracy. This is what makes cookie-cutter ideologies so dangerous. Dogmas promising to resolve all doubts and insecurities seem to lift us from our lonely subjective existence and link us to a larger purpose. Without a memetic map of our world, we would have no way of orienting ourselves. A fixed point—which is what a meme creates—helps us organize complex reality in much the same way that stereotypes save us from having to pay too much attention to details. "Even if the map is wrong, it fulfills its psychological function," Fromm notes, making sense of our world for us. This is why reason is so important for debunking harmful memes instead of mindlessly passing them along. When we become meme smart, we are less easily controlled by ideas in the air.

Donkeys and Elephants

POLITICAL PARTIES ARE MEME COMPLEXES that brand us into opposing groups. I've never been a partisan—I don't understand the two-party mind. Watching Ann Coulter, the conservative apparatchik, locking horns with comedian Bill Maher—who, as a libertarian, stands against partisanship on principle—is an exercise in civic aggression whose purpose pretty much eludes me. You'd think we were living on different planets: Planet Ann, where moms bake cookies, the NRA rocks, and real men don't get married (to one another), and Planet Bill, where nobody tells you what to do, everybody's smoking a reefer, and geeky-thin neckties are always cool since they help you get laid by peroxide blondes like Ann Coulter.

We're split into opposing camps and left wondering—if you're anything like me—how and why this happened. What makes one person a liberal and another a conservative? Our five-toned moral organ seems to explain it. You will remember that the first two sides of this organ—harm/care and justice/fairness—are *individualistic* ethics concerned with personal ethical treatment. The other three sides—in-group loyalty, authority/respect, and sacredness/purity— are *community* ethics intended to bind the group together. Where you stand on the partisan map depends on which of these five things you care about most.

Liberals care most about the individualistic ethics, harm/care and justice/fairness, according to Jonathan Haidt. Conservatives value these ethics as well, but give equal (or greater) importance to the binding community ethics. Social justice, the liberal ideal, is the ethic of autonomy writ large. But human cultures around the globe are overwhelmingly conservative, meaning that they empha- size the importance of all five moral protections. It is a minority, elitist thing to be liberal. What good are individual rights, conserva- tives ask, if the core values of group loyalty, traditional decency, and respect for authority are disregarded? As a rule, conservatives tend to be wary of the individualizing foundations because they are more pessimistic about human nature than liberals are—believing that, left to our own devices, humans will devolve into freethinking sin- ners. Conservatives are also, as their party label suggests, more averse to change than the rest of us. To a conservative, the historical survival of an institution or practice, be it marriage, monarchy, or the free market, creates a prima facie case that it has served some human need. "[Systems] which have existed over a long period of time have a reason and purpose inherent in them, a collective wis- dom incarnate in them, and the fact that we don't perfectly under- stand or cannot perfectly explain why they work is no defect in them but merely a limitation in us," the conservative apologist Irving Kristol believed. Tell that to a bride about to be burned.

Liberal and conservative tendencies can be influenced by geog- raphy. "Populations with long crowding histories, such as the Japa- nese, the Javanese, and the Dutch, for instance, emphasize tolerance, conformity, and consensus, while populations spread out over expanses of land with empty horizons tend to value privacy and freedom instead," de Waal reports. In the 2004 presidential race, the great majority of counties that voted for John Kerry were located near major waterways, where ports and cities are usually located and mobility and diversity are greatest (Kerry had a foreign-born wife, remember). Areas with less mobility and diversity, generally, had the more traditional five-foundation take on moral matters, and were likely to vote for George W. Bush. Generally, Americans tend toward the liberal position that personal fairness should trump in-group loyalty (the individualist ethic beats the communitarian) in matters of business, which is why nepotism and cronyism are verboten in the workplace. But other parts of the world think this is crazy. An Egyptian, for example, would want to know what self-respecting person would favor strangers over his own brother? Neither side is wrong.

In addition to the "horizontal" distinction between liberal and conservative, cultures also divide themselves "vertically" on a three-tiered ethical hierarchy. The first kind of culture is based on the *ethic of autonomy.* In societies like this, the moral world is assumed to be made up exclusively of individual human beings. The purpose of moral regulation, according to Jonathan Haidt and Jesse Graham, is to "protect the zone of discretionary choice of individuals and to promote the exercise of individual will in the pursuit of personal preferences." The second kind of culture is built on the *ethic of community.* Such cultures tend to see the world as a collection of institutions, families, tribes, guilds, or other groups. They view their ethical job as the moral protection of various stations or roles that constitute the society or community. Third, there are cultures based on the *ethic of divinity.* Haidt claims that in this sort of culture, which you find in countries like Saudi Arabia, "ethical life takes as its starting point the presumption of God's existence and the world being a place composed of souls housed in bodies." In cultures based on the ethic of divinity, morality is expected to ensure that the temple of the body, believed to house the divine within, will not be degraded. Sacred and elevating as this sounds on paper, cultures based on the ethic of divinity tend to be repressive, unprogressive, and cruel to females. Saudi women, for example, are proscribed from revealing their bodies in public as a means of protecting this rumored purity. In cultures predicated on divinity, public morality is a chastity belt tightened to help its citizens avoid sin by dictating whom they can sleep with, how often, and what they may eat, drink, and smoke—and on what days of the week—to ensure a place in paradise.

When you begin to tune your partisan ear, you realize how accurate this liberal-conservative theory is. You may even learn to appreciate, if not accept, values expressed by members of the opposite party. When you see that liberals are individualists, broadly speaking, and conservative are communitarians, first, the ethical edicts of the other side begin to make more sense. Just watch CNN for an hour and see if this isn't true. I tried this myself recently. The first program centered on xenophobic newsman Lou Dobbs, who was bloviating—again—against illegal immigration. I watched border-obsessed Lou going red in the face, but rather than hurling insults at the TV, angered by his zealous nationalism, I found myself understanding (if not liking), for the first time, where angry Lou was coming from. To a conservative, the homeland is sacred, making illegal immigrants immoral people. If laws are laws and sacrosanct, even against individual harm, it doesn't matter if the illegal Mexican alien has lived in this country for decades, raised a family here, paid taxes, and sent a son off to fight in an American war. Lou wants him to pack up his serape and go home.

Next, I tuned in to a panel dissecting the conundrum of same-sex marriage. I've always been able to understand why liberals support consensual adults in tying the knot in whatever blasphemous way they choose, but the conservative position has left me perplexed. Now, watching these righties and lefties have at it, the conservative view began to reveal its virtues—if not its veracity. When you've built your ethical life on tradition, institution, authority, and purity, as moral ideals, the prospect of unbridled carnal life (which includes homosexuality for most conservatives) becomes a natural, albeit phobic, reason to oppose gay marriage. For conservatives, marriage is not a personal choice, it's a problem for the state, church, and law books. The moral symbolism of same-sex coupling, I realized while watching these frightened Republicans, transcends the merely physical act of men sleeping with men, and women choosing women (however sickening that might be to them). I could hear the anti–gay pundits' gag reflex talking, disgust justifying itself with political rhetoric. I could hear this disgust *not* merely as homophobia but also as a longing for purity. I detected spiritual aspiration under their bigotry, a sincere belief in sacredness (as in "sacred union") being the only human antidote to wantonness here in the megabuffet of earthly temptations.

Then I changed the channel. The point is that both sides have a point. Neither team is completely wrong. As Haidt said in a 2008 lecture in Boulder, a person "can't just dismiss this stuff as social convention if you hope to understand human morality, and not just Western." For conservatives, the willingness to keep an open mind, revisit traditions, and to presume their fellows innocent before proven guilty (as in original sin) seem like useful places to start. For liberals, acknowledging that the individual isn't everything, that "do your own thing" is a glib, silly meme, and that customs like sexual restrictions, food taboos, and respect for leaders and gods (over personal concerns) are sometimes called for is probably a good idea. We need both individualizing *and* communitarian foundations to function in the world. We also need respect for authority.

The Higher
a Monkey Climbs,
the More You Can
See of Its Behind

[RESPECT/AUTHORITY]

Part Four

Independence of mind can have more than one
outcome; it may promise the philosopher but
deliver the tyrant.

—H. J. FORBES

Holy Shit

A FRIEND OF MINE ESCAPED FROM A CULT. This particular cult was the one organized around the Indian "holy" man Bhagwan Rajneesh in Oregon in the early 1980s. My buddy, Linda S., is a successful journalist and publisher today, but back then she was an unhappy, insatiable spiritual seeker who visited Rajneesh's ashram for a weekend workshop and wound up staying for two bizarre years. Rajneeshpuram was a vast, self-contained complex (group narcissism climaxes in cult behavior) spread out over a sixty-four-thousand-acre ranch in Oregon's Wasco County, near the state's northern border. The ashram was presided over by Bhagwan Rajneesh, a dangerously charismatic figure with swan-white hair, bedroom eyes, and a taste for kinky sex in the form of coerced copulation among his disciples, sometimes in the master's presence, husbands and wives forced to swap partners at the snap of his sacred fingers.

Eventually, Rajneesh would be run out of the country on multiple counts of immigration fraud, tax evasion, and sociopathic crimes, including the worst mass bioterrorism incident in U.S. history (his cronies had poisoned 751 Oregonians at local restaurants in order to steal a county election for the Rajneeshees). But when Linda was there, at least at first, mystic magic seemed to fill the Pacific air trailing Bhagwan's presence. "He really did have amazing spiritual gifts," Linda, a Jewish girl from Nashville, Tennessee, explains to me in her southern drawl when I ask why she stayed so long. "He could induce a kind of ecstasy in people."

"Drug induced?"

"Not only. He had charismatic powers. I believe he was half enlightened," she says. "But the other half was evil." When Linda talks about the experience, she sounds wonderstruck, distant, out of body. "It's hard to believe it really happened," she admits.

"You believed that he was holy?"

"I never completely bought into it. Not completely. I could see there was a gap between what was being said and what was real," says Linda, sounding like a reporter. "As the schism [between Rajneesh's power circle and ordinary devotees] got greater and greater, and the situation devolved, the power tripping got more intense." She tells me about women forced to sleep with other women's husbands "to break them of their egotistical attachment." Disciples—sounding more like prisoners in the Stanford Prison Experiment—"were also moved around from room to room to punish and manage us." As a freethinking woman of independent means, Linda was particularly threatening to this closed society and received especially harsh treatment, twelve-hour shifts in the kitchen, heavy lifting, and things she won't discuss in public. But why did she stay? "I was hypnotized by the drama," she says. "Watching it play out."

"Interesting word. Hypnotized."

"It was like that. The same as after 9/11. It was obvious that we were being lied to by the Bush government. Even though Bhagwan's people were denying it"—news of the poisoning and corruption cases were in the headlines by then—"all you had to do was breathe to know it was a lie."

As the guru's tyranny escalated, a rumor began to circulate that Bhagwan's innermost circle was planning to poison a group of the ashram's most dedicated members, including Linda herself. According to testimony by another ex-member, "a mass lethal poisoning of hundreds or thousands of neo-sannyasins was almost carried off one night, their lives spared only by an accident." As the state investigation widened, paranoia warped the atmosphere further. The resident nurse started giving out heavy meds, including Vicodin, to keep the inner circle sedated and obedient. "Bhagwan's secretary was this vicious, scary person. One day, she was so stoned that she passed out in a plate of spaghetti. It just got weirder and weirder. It was all unraveling from the inside."

Linda managed to escape from Rajneeshpuram in the nick of time, and began the long process of deprogramming. Evil authority nearly cost her her life, though, and that fact isn't easy to live with. In time, the brainwashing wore off and Linda returned fully to civilian life, wiser and more wary than before. Today, she's the founder of a thriving online newspaper and a contented mother of two. What shocks her the most, when she thinks about it, is that many of Bhagwan's disciples followed him back to India (after his pleas for asylum were turned down by twenty-one other countries), knowing what they knew about his corruption. "These were PhD's, doctors, lawyers. Very smart people! They just could not divorce themselves from that reality. They had too much invested in it. It was such a fringe society that it was hard to walk away from. There was no obvious bridge back to normal life. When you're caught in an upside-down place like that, morally speaking, it's harder to act on what you know you should do. It's hard in plain old daily life to act on what you know that you should do."

"That's the truth."

"But watching these people deny and rationalize what was going on—" Linda shakes her head. "I felt like I was seeing what had happened in Nazi Germany. Not wanting to admit that the dark underside exists."

Linda's story reminds me of an afternoon I spent listening to a group of male sexual perpetrators a few years back while researching a story on sexual abuse. These eight men and their female facilitator were assembled in a kindergarten classroom after school hours, which was creepy in itself, all those empty miniature chairs and crayon drawings covering the walls. This group of rapists was sitting in a circle, having their weekly meeting, telling hard-to-listen-to stories about daughters, stepdaughters, and employees they'd molested. Still, I'd expected to be more disgusted by these perps. My mind was full of judgment when I got there, like George Orwell going to war to fight the Fascists and then stumbling into the Spanish soldier with his pants falling down: just another human being. Seeing the ordinariness of these criminals caused a "sympathy breakthrough" in me; hearing their banal explanations of how the rapes had happened, I felt my condemnation shift. These were guys any of us could know, not monsters. These were men who'd slipped and done reprehensible things. I wasn't excusing them, not at all, but it was hard not to see their humanity, too (as the loyal Rajneeshees had done with their fallen leader, no doubt). One guy, who looked a lot like my father, was hardest for me not to have sympathy for. He had greased back hair and a tattoo on his forearm, and he talked about his stepdaughter's overattachment to him (her biological father had been physically abusive) and how beautiful their relationship had been. He'd helped to raise the girl and never till that night, when she was in the third grade, did he imagine that he could violate anyone. They were in the den, in their pj's, he said. Mom was away for the weekend. There was beer and tickling—then she threw herself into his lap and his body, he said, took over from there. "I couldn't stop it. It wouldn't stop." The man blinked back his tears when he said this. "I still can't believe that this happened. I loved this girl more than anything in the world."

The incest continued till she was sixteen. Finally, the teenager told her mother, who claimed not to have known what was going on. The man was arrested, did eighteen months in jail, had his wife divorce him, and was now, at forty-three, a convicted felon shunned by family and friends, forced to register himself as a sex offender in whatever community he chose to live in.

Later, I interviewed another teenage girl who had also been raped by her stepfather. "He seemed so sad," said the victim. "I loved him. I wanted him to be happy." To the eye of reason, this looks bonkers; to the eye of the heart, in spite of oneself, it is understandable that a child might lose herself in misconstrued empathy for an authority figure who should have known better. Traveling in Cambodia a few years back, Linda had a similar experience. She had gone there with a friend who arranged adoptions of Thai children. Linda realized that this friend of hers was having sex with kids in Thailand. "It was the same with Bhagwan," Linda tells me. "People like this are incredibly evil and really smart. My friend wasn't in conflict about it at all. It's a narcissistic characteristic. That capacity to damage other people with no conscience comes from believing that your reality is the only reality and that you're the only one who can be damaged."

Authority combined with Hungry Ghost ego corrupts a person absolutely. Unfortunately, we're hardwired to follow the leader, even when the leader is cruel or damaged, or intoxicated by being on top. Obedience can be a beautiful thing when leaders are trustworthy and conscientious. But when they're arrogant, greedy, aggressive people, evil is unleashed in the world. "We may not be certain what is at the heart of darkness, but we do know what keeps it beating—obedience," wrote Iris Makler.

The Dark Triad

J OSEPH STALIN WAS A CHARMER. People who met Uncle Joe were frequently over the moon about how charming this dictator was, with those bedroom eyes and great big mustache and how, when you sat close to him, it felt as if you were being pulled into a gigantic glove of fur, sympathy, protection, and specialness. Devils, of course, can be gentlemen.

Our species is haunted by three principal nemeses dubbed "the dark triad" by psychologists: Machiavellians, pathological narcissists, and psychopaths.

MACHIAVELLIANS

"A prince who wants to keep his authority must learn how not to be good, and use that knowledge, or refrain from using it, as necessity requires," Machiavelli wrote in his paean to wantonness, *The Prince*. Machiavellians—Machs for short—are people who will use whatever means they have at their disposal, including other people, to satisfy their needs and desires. In a pop test for this condition (you'll find a link to the Mach Test at the end of the book), in fact, statements from *The Prince* are used to determine a diagnosis. These range from "The biggest difference between most criminals and other people is that the criminals are stupid enough to get caught"—true or false?—to "Most people forget more easily the death of their parents than the loss of their property."

Machs have neither the capacity for, nor interest in, empathic connection. I-It arrangements are their métier. Machs typically have what's called "tunnel vision empathy," meaning that they can bring someone's emotions into focus when they wish to use that person, then tune them out once they have served their purpose. "They see the world in rational, probabilistic terms that are not only devoid of emotions but absent the ethical sense that flows from human concern," writes Barbara Oakley in her book *Evil Genes*. This is why Machs fall so easily into villainy; Machiavellian despots are far and away the type most responsible for "the mass murder century" just behind us.

We all have a little Mach inside us. Our culture is billboarded with Machiavellian slogans. Look out for number one. Failure is not an option. Winner take all. Nice guys finish last. (Indeed, some scientists believe that the winner-take-all aspect of American culture nurtures Dark Triadism, including psychopathy.) Machs believe it is better to be feared than loved. Strategy is everything; the world, to them, is a great blood-soaked chess game of connivers and liars covering their tracks and deceiving their way into people's hearts. I knew a Machiavellian once. He is the only genuinely evil soul I've ever had the misfortune to know. I wasn't acquainted with him for long; we were friends from college, and he was fun-loving company. I didn't know that he was a drug dealer and pimp, till one day I found an enormous rock of heroin in the bottom of his linen closet. This was followed by the death of his drug-dealing brother at the hands of a knife-wielding gang in a Thai jail. My Mach "friend" lied about these details without a flinch. Then his lies fell apart; I confronted him, he continued to lie, and I broke off relations. But, oh, was he a cool character! And suave as a gigolo working a room. You could have skied off how slippery he was.

Machs never consider their ends to be selfish or evil; rather, they invent a convincing rationale and justify their tyranny by the need to protect the state, the bank account, whatever. There's a curdling story about how a group of Mach SS men behaved at the Nuremberg Trials. "They found a remarkable solution to the problem of how to present themselves," Lance Morrow writes. "They felt sorry for themselves. They marinated in self-pity and self-cherishing; they fairly caramelized themselves in sentimentality. They solved their formidable moral problem by declaring themselves the injured party." Perpetrators once again absolved themselves of guilt by donning the victim's mask.

NARCISSISTS

While all Machs are narcissists, not all narcissists are Machs. These two delightful personality types share self-absorption, lack of empathy, and moral retardation (they're stuck somewhere in tyrannical infancy), but narcissists are not necessarily evil people. They're vain and deluded, but not always evil. Machs smell sulphuric after a while—you know you're with the morally dead—but narcissists fly more easily under our ethical radar. Our culture rampantly encourages narcissism, after all—one more Botox commercial and *all* our laugh lines will freeze—making narcissists, who are often charismatic and attractive people, even harder to identify. Narcissists can seem benign and happy-go-lucky even in relationships. Their emotional immaturity and inability to love can be interpreted as garden-variety cluelessness, especially if they are men.

Narcissists, like the god in the myth, tend to be more egotistically fragile than Machs, desperate when they lose the spotlight, confused and angry when people leave them, unable to grasp that their psychological illness has installed in their minds a one-way mirror, reflecting themselves back ad infinitum. You may have seen the film *Being John Malkovich,* in which the director ventures inside the movie star's head and finds thousands of John Malkoviches everywhere he looks—big surprise!—his own squinty-eyed self in centriplicate. My favorite description of how narcissism operates comes from psychiatrist Mark Epstein's book *Thoughts Without a Thinker,* a study of psychoanalysis and Buddhist thought. In discussing our modern predicament, which includes large doses of narcissism, Epstein describes the polarities between which the narcissistic personality swings. He deserves to be quoted at length:

> They are, in fact, the two poles of the false self: namely, the grandiose self developed in compliance with the parents' demands and in constant need of admiration, and the empty self, alone and impoverished, alienated and insecure, aware only of the love that was never given. The grandiose self, while fragile and dependent on the admiration of others, believes itself to be omnipotent or self sufficient and so retreats into aloofness or remoteness, or, when threatened, clings to an idealized other from whom it hopes to retrieve its power. The empty self clings in desperation to that which it feels can assuage its hollowness or retreats to a barren void in which it is unapproachable and which reinforces the belief in its own worthlessness. Neither feels entirely satisfactory, but to the extent that we are governed by the demands of the false self, we can envision no alternative.

Grandiosity and emptiness. This is the narcissist's dilemma. He is both omnipotent and spectral, all-powerful in his imagination and powerless without admirers to feed his illusion of plenitude. This paradoxical quality in narcissists, of being both unbearable in their selfishness and poignant in their self-doubt, is part of what keeps us in their thrall.

I used to work for the pop artist Andy Warhol as an editor at *Interview* magazine, the mecca of narcissistic wannabes (and superstars) who lived for their fifteen minutes of fame. As an editor responsible for stoking the exhibitionist machine, I found it poignant to watch what happened to major narcissists after their quarter hour of spotlight time was over. The fall from grandiosity to emptiness came with a splat for one starlet who'd been especially gorgeous, globally lauded for her Pre-Raphaelite looks, and whose vehement insecurity only made her more sympathetic as the light dimmed over the years and the star machine left her stranded behind. She now roams the streets of my neighborhood with her head swathed in Hermès scarves, shielded by stupendous sunglasses, a trench coat up to her chin, her once-beautiful face a construction zone of surgeries (by the dozen) gone wrong, moving ethereally through the streets like the shade of Persephone in Purgatory, caught between the painful twin cravings to be seen and to disappear. There's nothing more empty than fame, as we all know in the TMZ age, but seeing the celebrity thresher from the inside out, how it sucked people in, gutted them, and left them for dead, taught me a lot about how narcissism perpetuates itself and also why narcissists suffer. Because they do suffer. Remember that routine by the mime Marcel Marceau, where he puts a mime mask over his face and then can't manage to pry it off? This is what I think of every time I pass this aging starlet in the street. Grotesque attention is better than none.

Machiavellians and narcissists can produce great things. Remember the Buddhist notion of near-enemies? Machiavellianism is the near-enemy of heroic singleness of purpose, if not necessarily for the greater good. The near-friend of narcissistic grandiosity is the ability to inspire unshakable confidence in time of need, when all eyes are on the narcissist in charge. "Where would we be today if Churchill, who once claimed that 'megalomania is the only form of sanity,' hadn't turned his mighty narcissism into resistance against Hitler's advance?" Barbara Oakley asks. "It was Churchill's convincing, egotistically certain manner that rallied the troops and the populace around the idea of standing fast rather than continuing with fruitless appeasement, as Lord Halifax was wont to do." Character flaws such as stubbornness, insatiability, and self-centeredness can, hitched to a higher star, become virtues that transcend merely selfish aims, she asserts. So long as megalomaniacs are willing to brook disagreement, and change course when it's appropriate, their obsessive energy can be used for the good.

PSYCHOPATHS

Psychopaths are the deepest end of the Dark Triad swimming pool. A distressed mother of a psychopathic child described the appearance and worsening of her child's mental health:

> At eighteen months, it was as if a switch had gone off in him. He started showing tremendous rage, complete lack of remorse and an almost complete lack of empathy. His first reaction, when he would see an animal, would be to kill it. He became extremely hateful and vicious. The mother went on to describe his predatory . . . behavior toward her, including starting fires in the house, threatening her with a knife, and sticking straight pins out of the carpet in front of her dresser . . . Once he hanged a cat in the backyard and waited for his mother to come home to watch her reaction.

She remembers seeing his pleasure at her horror, and then imitating her horror back to her.

Psychopathy is more common in men than women. The psychopathy checklist created by psychologist Robert Hare includes twenty items, such as parasitic lifestyle, pathological lying, conning, proneness to boredom, shallow emotions, lack of empathy, poor impulse control, promiscuity, irresponsibility, and prison record. Psychopaths tend to be intelligent, unreliable, dishonest, irresponsible, self-centered, emotionally shallow, and lacking in insight. Among their most disturbing features is awareness of what they're doing—their clear awareness of right and wrong. Unfortunately, these are mere rhetorical concepts and have little or no effect on their actions in real contexts. As Aristotle counseled, knowledge alone is rarely enough to change moral behavior. A person has to *feel* something.

Psychopaths are unable to recognize threat, even when threats are aimed at them. Irregularity in their amygdalas and related brain circuits cause them to respond paradoxically to danger. Psychopaths about to receive an electrical shock show no sign of the fear response that is normal in people about to experience pain. Because the prospect of pain does not trigger a surge of anxiety, psychopaths lack concern about future punishments for what they do. Unlike the neurological response of normal people, when psychopaths' anger mounts, their heart rate drops instead of climbing. They grow calmer the more dangerous, or endangered, they become, according to Marc Hauser: "The presence of a potential victim is as tempting to the psychopath as is a drink to an alcoholic, a slot machine to a gambler, or a piece of chocolate to a young child." Unable to recognize submissive clues, without empathy and the feeling of aversiveness that comes from detecting distress, nothing prevents them from doing harm. It is an emotional impairment, not a rational one.

We have somatic markers to help us recognize psychopaths. The sensation of crawling skin is our limbic disgust response to the absence of emotional cuing and normalcy we detect in such miscreants. Psychopaths like Bhagwan Rajneesh have the ability to disguise their sickness under a holy veneer. These criminally minded manipulators tap into what may be the human race's greatest moral frailty: spiritual hunger. Meher Baba, a genuine spiritual master who died in 1969, described this in a trenchant essay called "Spiritual Jingoism." "The whole world is pining for light and freedom," Meher Baba wrote.

> To meet this recurrent and poignant demand there always arises a plentiful supply of those who claim to meet it adequately. Most of these claimants are impostors . . . The temptation to seize the ideal imaginatively and pose as having realized it is so irresistible that there are very few who do not succumb to it. This is the origin of the fraudulent saint or the spiritual jingo, who walks and talks with his nose in the air and arms akimbo as if he were somebody very special.

How else could Rajneesh have compared Mohandas Gandhi to Adolf Hitler with a straight face—and actually think he was making sense? In a ludicrous attempt to equate goodness with evil, Rajneesh—in a teaching against self-mortification—called Gandhi as much of a "violent torturer" as Hitler. "To torture oneself or to torture others, both are diseases," he actually claimed. "Somebody is an Adolf Hitler, he tortures others. Somebody is a Mahatma Gandhi, he tortures himself. *Both are in the same boat* [italics mine], maybe standing back to back, but standing in the same boat."

The mind reels at such ignorance. Rajneesh repeated: "Adolf Hitler's joy is in torturing others, Mahatma Gandhi's joy is in torturing himself, but both are violent. The logic is the same—their joy depends on torture." Only a very sick mind could actually believe this. The clue to Rajneesh's mental illness lies in his use of the word "logic"; to a psychopath, logic is everything. Torture the mind with thoughts, torture bodies with starvation, it's all the same hellish hullabaloo. That's samsara! And besides, who cares? It's all just semantics, anyway. In a world psychopathically stripped of emotion, nothing signifies or has real substance. Having no substance, it cannot matter.

Evil

THE MYTH OF PURE EVIL is just as illusory as the myth of absolute goodness. Though moralists loathe this mixed-up truth, we can't avoid recognizing that the potential for redemption exists in nearly every villain. You'll rarely find a monstrous soul who doesn't love something or who does not, in whatever trivial way, have the capacity for benevolence. The question of whether people are evil or their deeds are evil is a parlor game for judges, priests, and philosophers. Experts quibble over whether an objective measure of evil exists, or whether evil is quantifiable only in the jaded eye of the beholder. "Would evil exist in a universe from which human beings were absent?" Lance Morrow has asked. "Male Kodiak bears eat the cubs toddling down from their winter dens. Why do such acts by humans have dire moral meaning, theological significance, while among animals, they have none? What sermons about mankind's inherent evil would we inflict upon ourselves if human males were in the habit of seizing and eating newborn babies on their way home from the hospital?"

The naturalistic fallacy aside, this question has philosophical merit. No universally forbidden behavior exists on this planet. Incest, murder, cannibalism, and rape, though denounced by nearly everybody, are also always practiced and sanctioned somewhere; and, in the case of rape, are a requirement for membership in certain exclusive men's clubs. During the Bosnian war, if a Serb soldier refused to rape, he could be shot by his comrades. Rape bonded men in atrocity. Some Serb men forced Muslim men to use their teeth to castrate their own sons, and sons to castrate their fathers. The evil of rape is a medal of honor in the consensus reality of certain nations. We shift the margins of sane behavior, protected by moral dumbfounding. But can evil actually be judged by sensibilities and instinctive revulsion? No. Blacks were lynched because they disgusted whites, not because they were disgusting. If evil cannot be judged by the sensibilities and the instinctive revulsion we feel, is there some more objective, rational measurement? Or is evil finally just a matter of taste, and *de gustibus non est disputandum*? It's impossible to dispute taste.

Think of the archetype of the fool. Fools have an interesting link to evil and where we draw its parameters. The ancient archetype of the fool is defined by opposites merging in the same individual. The nonduality of fools makes them wise precisely because they transcend categories, as we learn from Shakespeare's plays. It was the mission of the holy fool to point out hypocrisy (evil embedded in goodness—goodness embedded in evil) and promote harmony and goodwill by demonstrating what a mixed bag each of us really is, a congeries of evil and kindness. We see this synthesis of good and evil in many wisdom traditions, where the greatest saints—like the Tibetan murderer-turned-holy-man, Milarepa—break down moralistic barriers in pursuit of a deeper, eternal truth. (There is some of this in the Christian figure of whore-turned-divine-handmaiden, Mary Magdalene.) In Buddhist and Hindu iconography, divine figures are often depicted with demons attached to their bodies, indicating that evil is inseparable from good. Opposites are also melded in the image of the "sacred androgyne" found throughout history, which combined male and female principles into a hybrid third form of wisdom (such as Shiva Ardhanarishvara, the androgynous deity composed of Shiva and his consort, Shakti). While ignorant people see everything in black and white, and rely on the myth of pure evil, the wise look beyond oversimplification.

I love what Aleksandr Solzhenitsyn says about this in *The Gulag Archipelago*: "If only there were evil people somewhere insidiously committing evil deeds and it were necessary only to separate them from the rest of us and destroy them. But the line dividing good and evil cuts through the heart of every human being. And who is willing to destroy a piece of his own heart?" It is much less scary to think of someone like Jeffrey Dahmer, the serial anthropophagite (he liked to kill and eat young boys), as a monster of pure evil than it is to call him a man gone wrong. It's easier to electrocute a monster than a man; language, words like "pure evil," can barricade us from the ambiguous nigglings of conscience.

The confounding truth about human nature is that people commit evil (or permit evil) not because of some great malevolence, but for mundane reasons ranging from conformity and convenience to jingoism and cowardice. It is interesting to learn that violence and cruelty have four main causes. Greed is first, not surprisingly. Ambition is second—ditto. Third, cruelty comes from sadism, which is relatively rare. But the most destructive behavior, by far, comes from reputedly "good" aspects of character—high self-esteem, moral idealism, and so on. When someone's self-esteem is unrealistic or narcissistic, however, so-called virtues can lead to violence. All it takes for evil to flourish is the belief that *your* violence is justified.

Our prejudiced calculations of right and wrong, good and bad, can be applied by callous dictators and obedient functionaries alike with a broad, undiscriminating brush that neutralizes killing with the appearance of justice—of unavoidable, vaguely benevolent acts, at least. "The only thing necessary for evil to triumph is for good men to do nothing," as we know from Irish politician and philosopher Edmund Burke. I learned this lesson myself a few years ago on a subway platform. I was waiting for a train some distance away from a woman and a chubby boy of about ten. The woman seemed unstable—her voice went from a normal tone to near screaming—before she pushed the boy to the ground and began kicking him in the stomach, yelling at him as he lay there, trying to protect himself. It happened so fast, and I was so far down the platform, that I did nothing. I still can't believe it. I stood there watching this crazy woman attack her son, and was ready to interfere, but felt paralyzed by some don't-interfere-in-family-matters voice in my head. Suddenly, the train appeared and the incident ended. I've been ashamed of this moment ever since. I was certainly complicit with evil by doing nothing.

Someone else who was troubled by cruelty—but didn't stand on the sidelines—is Jared Miller, a colleague of mine from V-Day, an organization that works to end violence against women and girls. In 2006, Miller, a thirty-year-old black man, left his partnership with a private equity firm in Nashville, Tennessee, gave away his belongings, and moved to Rwanda. At the time, Jared was a party boy gone sour on the singles circuit. "I was drinking too much, very unhappy," Jared tells me. "I'd truly reached the end of my rope." Driven by a "never-ending hunger for something more that I needed to feed," this financial analyst turned his money-raising acumen to humanitarian use by teaching business skills to abused women struggling to feed their families. War-torn Rwanda may be second only to the Democratic Republic of Congo in brutality against women in Africa. Unmarried Rwandan women are often sold into the sex trade, and Jared was determined to help these women attain the freedom they deserved.

Three days after setting foot on African soil, Jared met a group of twenty-three prostitutes, all of whom were determined to find a way out of their degrading profession. "Most of them had been sexually abused since childhood, conditioned to believe they were worthless," Jared tells me. "The majority of them had multiple children as a result of years of rape. They were living through hell on earth—with evil in control—and needed to find a way out."

He bonded immediately with a woman named Virginia and her two young daughters, three-year-old Deborah and one-year-old Gigi. "They were so captivating, so pure, so unsuspecting, and seemingly happy despite the tragic reality surrounding them," he says. "In Deborah, I saw innocence and beauty like I'd never witnessed before. Everything changed for me from that moment on. Somehow, my fight for this cause had culminated in leading me to this precious little girl. Everything became real and human for me. My fight was no longer for a cause—it was for her and all those like her. I could not bear to see her suffer. Deborah's six now and represents everything I'm fighting for. She is the heart line that drives me."

Today, Jared's group of women has grown to forty (with over a hundred children). He travels the world raising support for them, selling their handmade jewelry and telling their stories. "I try to provide a window into their lives. I ask people in the States what they would do for their own daughter to protect and care for her. Would they do the same for their niece or their neighbor's daughter? What about a little African girl?" In other words, how removed must we be from suffering in order to dissociate?

Where does responsibility stop? Do we collaborate with evil by ignoring it? Are we hurting the dispossessed of the world when we—consumers in a global marketplace—wear our Gap T-shirts sewn by underpaid minors in brown-skinned countries? As increasingly global beings, we find ourselves in ethical overwhelm. That's not because we're cowards and wusses, or First World snobs more preoccupied with our cappuccinos than decapitations in Afghanistan; it's not because we are inherently evil ourselves and therefore accomplices to bad things we don't try to stop. It's because we're not emotionally wired to save the world. We're wired to save the neighborhood—and not even the *whole* hood, just our family and a surrounding enclave of a hundred or so other people. Global man feels called upon to be an animal he hasn't become yet, capable of Web empathy, TV empathy, empathy for generations of people to whom we hope not to bequeath a barren and toxic planet. Global man's mandate is enormous, and necessary, and pushing us to the adaptation fast track. But despite our great wealth of information, we are not globally empathic yet.

Knowing this matters if we want to cultivate a realistic view of evil. The standards for measuring ethical behavior are becoming more abstract by the day. It's evil to be fat, for instance, if you believe what you read in magazines. "Possessing an excessive carbon footprint is rapidly becoming the modern equivalent of wearing a scarlet letter," *The New Yorker* reported recently. Studies suggest that "the biggest problem arising from the epidemic of obesity is the additional carbon burden that fat people—who tend to eat a lot of meat and travel mostly in cars—place on the environment." If your Big Mac and Hummer are burning up the ozone layer that will or will not allow life to survive on the planet, is it functionally evil to be fat? How about secondhand smoke? Are you evil if your children get asthma from your habit? Are you evil if you sell guns or booze or any of the other millions of things that people die from? Where does the responsibility stop? Where do we draw the compassion line? Are we responsible for the whole world?

We feel secretly miffed while recycling our trash, annoyed that the violence *out there* never ends, increasingly numbed by the density of grief. From all sides, the Guilt Fascists, Food Fascists, Fur Fascists, Smoke Fascists, and P.C. Fascists assault us with the growing list of crimes of which we are guilty simply by being alive in the First

World. At a recent dinner party, one of my more radical friends was so offended by my ordering the Chilean sea bass that she delivered a lecture on overfished species and the selfishness of gastronomic gluttony (she had ordered the tortellini, apparently not an endangered pasta). Imagine how such guilt tripping would sound to an ancient Sumerian come back from the dead. Such a time-traveling man would have played two, maybe three roles in his entire life (we play dozens); his worldly and ethical concerns would have centered around a head of cattle, a bow and arrow, a libido, a family, and a handful of local human connections. Being transported into the present day, thrust into modern man's multitasking, multiethnic, beleaguered, and fretful conscience would be devastating. How long would it take for the flummoxed Sumerian to go nuts, do you think, untangling this complex web of concerns? How quickly would he be lopping this too-big world, with its too many moral demands and afflictions, into manageable guilt-free chunks—not my problem, not my problem—in order to feel okay about himself? Could he distinguish right from wrong in this confusing mess of cares? The Sumerian would be completely *meshuga*. How good can any of us possibly be on a shrinking planet that's heating up faster than you can say hydrofluorocarbons? The truthful answer: very. That's part of what makes us so insecure about our own moral worth.

Eve Ensler has just written a play about a privileged New York woman so guilt-ridden over her material advantages, so freighted down with O.P.C. (Obsessive Political Correctness), that she's reduced to becoming a "freegan"—a Dumpster diver who rescues food from trash cans and will eat only what's been thrown away. Her main character wears dresses sewn together from the skins of discarded fruit ("What is that? Tangerine? Oh, I love it!"). It's a serious bitch being affluent.

When authority is honorable rather than evil, disrespect toward that authority is morally noxious to us. We are wired to respect our elders for profound and beautiful reasons. The dismal state of marriage and family as institutions has fractured our notion of filial piety, but in traditional cultures there is no moral offense greater than disrespecting—or harming, killing, or usurping the power of—a beloved chief or family elder. Imagine an episode of the *Jerry Springer Show,* or *Dr. Phil,* or some reality show where children are trashing their parents on national TV—then consider what the Buddha said about respect. According to him, we could carry our parents on our shoulders for the rest of their lives and still not repay the gift of our precious human birth. Such gratitude and respect sound quaint to our post-Freudian ears. Authority has become a loaded concept; corruption in high places has all but eroded our built-in propensity for reverence, our moral hunger for role models and belief in our leaders—not to mention parents. "I didn't ask to be born!" teenagers complain when their allowance runs out and their hormones run high. Abuse of authority has warped our gratitude. We are also deprived of the wisdom of elders.

In primitive society, authority figures did not earn group members' respect through power grabbing and crude dominance (these Machiavellian qualities came later with enlarging, more densely populated societies). "Generosity and modesty [are] required of persons of high status in primitive society, and the rewards they receive are merely the love or attentiveness of others," Fromm writes. A potential chief needed to be "stronger, faster, braver, and more intelligent than any other member of the band." But that didn't guarantee him higher status. "Prestige [would] be accorded him only if these qualities are put to the service of the group. In primitive human society, greater strength must be used in the service of the community. The person, to earn prestige, must literally sacrifice to do so, working harder for less food." Tell that to the guys at AIG.

In fact, evil—especially as it relates to power—is nearly always a mix of narcissistic motives and idealism gone wrong. It is the rare psychopath who embodies evil deliberately and without reason. If you had asked Hitler, even he would have told you that he was working in service to the good. Does delusion excuse evil acts? Of course not. But it can help us become more "evil smart." The Baal Shem Tov, who founded Jewish Hasidism in eighteenth-century Poland, had an allegorical dream about this that I find wonderful. In the dream, this holy man (who compared enlightenment to walking out through the back door of his own mind) was confronted by the very incarnation of the evil impulse in the form of a sinister heart. The Baal Shem Tov seized the heart, in the dream, and pounded it furiously in hopes of destroying evil and redeeming the world. As he pummeled the heart, he suddenly heard an infant's sobbing coming from its depths. In the dream, he stopped beating the heart, realizing that in the midst of evil is a voice of innocence. He realized that "there is goodness entangled in evil."

Playing with Power

I T'S WORTH TAKING A STROLL DOWN evolution's memory lane if we want to understand how humans developed our problematic relationship to dominance and submission.
Anatomically modern humans appeared at the end of the Pale-
olithic era, about two hundred thousand years ago. These ancestors
grouped together into small-scale bands and societies, and gained
their subsistence from gathering plants and hunting wild animals.
Stone Age men produced the earliest works of art, engaged in religious and spiritual behavior (including burial and ritual), nursed
their elderly, assisted their cripples, and enjoyed lives both bucolic
and peaceful by our hectic, expansionist standards.

At the end of the last Ice Age, our species spread farther across
the earth. Sea levels rose around the planet, presenting a need to
adapt to the changing environs and discover new sources of food.
Agriculture was adopted during this Neolithic revolution, bringing
with it the invention of gardening, and pottery for carrying water
and seed. In the days before the agricultural revolution, our ancestors' existence was fairly egalitarian, anthropologists tell us. But as

humans became more hierarchical with the ability to trade (and make war), dominance became a less avoidable aspect of daily life. As tribal groups formed, headed by charismatic individuals—a big man, proto chief, or matriarch who functioned as head of the lineage—intergroup conflict and control of labor increasingly became more common.

Populations increased tenfold in density over those of hunter-gatherer societies. With clan members hunkering down on small plots of land, village life expanded, bringing with it job-specific divisions of labor among specialized craftspeople, merchants, soldiers, and so on. Thriving on agricultural surpluses, these chiefdoms grew into states where power was monopolized by hereditary leaders and members of the priestly castes. Ancient, democratic ethical codes were gradually transformed into dominating systems of regulation that always advantaged the ruling classes. It was around this time that humans originated the idea of lawgiving gods whose commands, not surprisingly, lent these ethical codes overpowering authority in the interests of the rulers.

We underestimate the existential shift that agriculture caused in our evolution as a species. With the ability to plant and harvest seed, human wherewithal increased many thousandfold. We ceased being wandering hunter-gatherer tribes and became, if not quite masters of the universe, masters-in-training for future conquest. Our self-image was altered irrevocably; we became creatures able to dominate the earth. The ability to make seeds grow with predictable results gave rise to an entirely new concept, Fromm tells us: "Man recognized that he could use his will and intention and make things happen, instead of things just happening." Within a short period, historically speaking, man learned to harness the physical energy of oxen and the energy of the winds. He invented the plough, the wheeled cart, and the sailing boat, and he perfected the chemical processes involved in the smelting of copper ores. He mastered the physical properties of metals and began to work out a solar calendar. With these major advances, small villages of self-sufficient farmers were transformed into populous cities (later city-states) nourished by secondary industries and foreign trade.

The invention of self-made, tillable land introduced a moral scourge to our species: human slavery. The land that needed tilling required a great deal of human labor, and this form of need for capital marked a sharp moral plunge, with the discovery that humans could be used for purely economic purposes and the resulting introduction of exploitation and slavery. The first consequence of slavery was the rise of different classes—a new phenomenon for humans. The privileged classes did the directing and organizing, claiming and obtaining for themselves a disproportionately large part of the product, and a standard of living that the majority of the population could not afford. This was more than an uptick in human production: It created a whole new set of social ideals. "There is a great difference between cultures which foster and encourage greed, envy, and exploitativeness by their social structure, and cultures which do the opposite," Fromm goes on. The exertion of power became the essence of civilization, which fueled itself on dominance, conquest, and rigorous—often cruel—forms of servitude. A by-product of this slave-driven way of life was the invention of war as an essential requisite to the accumulation of communal capital. You can't have an urban revolution without mountains of cash, and you can't procure funds without conquering others.

This is important to understand. Although we've always been aggressive and shared a carnivorous taste for bloodsport, it was not until the Neolithic period that men became barbarians. Our primitive progenitors were far *less* violent than our species would eventually become. The lower agriculturalists, hunters, and collectors were the least aggressive, and the highest pastoralists and hunters the most warlike. This inverts the outdated picture of human nature as evolving from primitive to civilized. In fact, sociologists attribute warmongering to civilization more than to belligerent animal nature. The more division of labor there is in a society, the more warlike it is, with class-system societies being the most warlike of all peoples.

History shows that men have always dominated women, though the quality of this dominance has shifted across time and between cultures. Proponents of gynocracy blame patriarchy for the rise of violence and these feminists may well be right. Unfortunately, this is a bit like claiming, as my sailor-mouthed mother used to say, that if the queen had balls she would be king. History records not a single society in which women have controlled the political and economic lives of men; even when queens have ruled, their intermediaries have remained primarily male. Since no record exists of a culture ruled by women, contrary to the myth of matriarchies past, where no blood was shed and everyone had a seat at the table, we have no idea what a world ruled by women would look like. Our fantasy of female rule may be little more than hypothesis; I know many greedy, power-mongering, hostile women who like nothing more than to dominate at the office, at home, in bed, and elsewhere. Carol Gilligan's conviction about women's different ethical judgment meter (care and connection versus dominance and justice) suggests that a female-dominated society might well be a more inclusive one, but this remains speculation. I would certainly like to see.

With agricultural dominance came a sea change in how humans viewed themselves. "*No longer the womb, but the mind became the creative power* [italics mine] . . . Man had overcome his inability for natural creation, a formerly female quality," in Fromm's words. With this leap to patriarchal power came a whole new kind of society, no longer democratic, neighborly, and egalitarian, but organized around a central, sometimes brutal, authority figure. Patriarchy led to the need for conquest and the trespassing of other groups' land and pillaging for profit and power. This conquistador approach fostered tyranny. That's the meaning of Saint Bonaventure's dictum that "the higher a monkey climbs, the more one sees of its behind." The fewer our social constraints—and the more power we hold—the more vain and reckless we're likely to become on our egotist's trapeze. People in power spend a lot of time figuring out how not to lose it, particularly if they were oppressed themselves. I know a woman like that. Having suffered parental abuse as a child, she later became a hellion herself, a serious, mean-mouthed, bitch on wheels. Remember Faye Dunaway in the film *Network*, as the power drunk TV executrix so profit-crazy that she checked her voice mail while having sex? The woman I know is a viper like that. I saw with my own eyes what controlling a vast business empire did to her already voracious greed. She'd have auctioned off her own mother for the right price.

Reality merges with fantasy inside a tyrant's bubble of privilege. The power tripper has no check on his or her will. The sycophants around them make it worse. Power is relational, after all, not an isolated attribute; we do have *some* say in how much power we give others. For every megalomaniac, there are underlings propping up his or her legend, shoveling flattery into their ego-pits. Submissives and dominants have a collusive arrangement and no one is more acutely aware of this than the alpha dogs themselves. That's what makes tyrants sit down extra hard on the people they need most. Still, we can deprive them of worship. There are ethical ways of rebelling against despotic treatment. We can choose to withdraw emotional support. We can take an inward step away from these difficult people and unplug ourselves from their vampiric demands. Respect and sycophancy are different. It's not our job to wipe their bottoms. Our job is to maintain self-respect.

One Up, One Down

WITH POWER CONCENTRATED AROUND a central authority, different means of organization were developed to keep people in line. In order for groups to cooperate, selfishness had to be regulated. There are two general approaches to how this can be done. They are called the *beehive* approach and the *contractual* approach. The contractual approach takes the individual as the fundamental unit of value. To build a contractual morality, all you need are the first two ethical concerns: harm/care and fairness/reciprocity. Contractualists are committed to reinventing institutions and fine-tuning laws in order to increase individual happiness and minimize suffering as circumstances change. By contrast, the beehive approach "takes the group and its territory as [the] fundamental sources of value," as Haidt puts it. "Individual bees are born and die by the thousands, but the hive lives a long time, and each individual has a role in fostering its success."

Beehives represent a traditional, orderly world where people share a vigorously enforced moral code and roles allow individuals to trust one another. But where contractual societies tend to be forward thinking and innovative, beehives risk sinking into conservatism and rigid forms of patriarchy. We appear to have the need for both approaches. Most of us are aware of this dichotomy in our own personalities, being drawn to both company and solitude. We are both individualistic, as metaphor-loving, brain-heavy, sentient creatures fascinated by our own existence, and gregariously hive-bound in wanting to hook arms and comb through the world. This helps to explain the betwixt-between feelings we have in life; how easily torn we are between interdependence and self-absorption. We want to couple but not all the time. We want to be surrounded but also left to ourselves. Couples desire to be left alone together but also need other couples for company. We want both freedom and limitation, which helps explain, too, our tendency to cling to bad situations too long. We're honey-glued together and can't fly away. We want to leave but something sticks us. It's not just because we're codependent (though we probably are), it's also because something in us doesn't want to leave the bee's nest. When the hive becomes too suffocating, though, we're likely to become depressed. Existential dread is nearly always linked to the feeling of being atomized. When collective interests subordinate the individual, we suffer from what Emile Durkheim termed "anomie," the state of feeling like "a disorganized dust of individuals." Modern people spend more time alone, or isolated in nuclear families, than we're biologically wired for, apparently. According to evolutionary psychologists, our amount of aloneness is completely unnatural.

Hierarchies may be understood as places where contractualists and beehives meet. We have the structure of a hive, and fixed roles and traditions, as well as a degree of individual autonomy, unless the hierarchy is run by power freaks. There's a sense of belonging to a collective, fulfilling a role required by the whole, but there's also upward mobility, unless you've got a lousy boss. In the collective, we get to be other people. Stepping into hierarchical roles, however, it's disturbing how vigorously some bureaucrats defend their tiny plot of turf, abusing roles they barely deserve. There's a special rung in hell for bureaucrats. I had a miserable experience recently with a hellish bureaucrat, a woman so heinously full of herself you'd have choked her if you had the chance. She stood between me and a serious thing in my life. This bureaucratic bimbo would not bend. The rules were the rules. She lived to say no—it was her drug of choice. Now, thank God, she's history. Anyone who's worked in a great bureaucracy himself (or seen the film *Metropolis*) knows there's nothing more life-sucking, dehumanizing, deindividualizing, and claustrophobic than sitting in a cubicle at an office of a corporation, munching your Doritos and wanting to implode.

"Two children pretending that a stick is a horse have taken their first step . . . toward inhabiting human institutional reality," Michael Tomasello tells us. Bureaucrats function ex cathedra behind the power of the institution. As Lily Tomlin used to say, playing Ernestine, the lip-sucking, switchboard-operating, eye-scrunching, bureaucrat meany with a bun in a hairnet, you can blame it on the phone company. "We don't have to," Ernestine used to tell her customers, meaning *have to give a damn,* "we're the phone company." Comedy aside, underneath the officious masks worn by bureaucrats hides the knowledge of their own replaceability. Many bureaucrats deal with this insecurity by cultivating passive aggression. They don't make the rules, they just bend them.

Though indispensable, hierarchies can also be corrupting for ambitious people. Backstabbing, looking out for numero uno, jockeying for favor, lunging for advancement, deceiving for advancement, moving ever upward—the incessant push for power and status—helps to fill the void of meaninglessness with the cotton balls of titles and roles. These roles are transitory, though, and empty of lasting significance. I once worked for a large New York corporation, with thousands of people in a sleek new high-rise, side by side by side in rows of identical windowless offices. I was only a temp there, luckily, but the Archie Bunker look-alike in the next office had been working for this corporation for forty years and given it the best years of his life. One morning, I arrived before he did and found his belongings packed into four white boxes outside his locked office door. This guy's position had evaporated overnight; the corporation had a new guard, and had simply thrown out this loyal servant like yesterday's garbage. It was immoral, tragic to witness, and dozens of hierarchical niches beyond the employee's power to change.

Bureaucrats often live in fear of losing their foothold in the uphill climb. I know because I did it myself. When I arrived in New York after college, my dream was to climb a magazine masthead until I was at the top. It mattered to my competitive ego. When I landed a desirable job, I felt I'd caught a lucky break, an updraft by the seat of my pants, and didn't care too much about the people I stepped over. I wasn't dishonest, just back-watching; I worked my guts out and got a good role—which I almost instantly started to hate. But in the beginning, the thrill of the climb was irresistible and inseparable from the rules of a snake's nest. You didn't really know who your friends were. The preferred topic of conversation was the boss, of course—a bombastic woman in fake Chanel suits, a benevolent (but not that benevolent) despot whom we both adored and despised. The rancor, suspicion, hypercompetitiveness, insecurity, hostility, and malice displayed by this hierarchy-crazed bunch of publishing bees, secretly and behind your back, was enough to make you hate magazines. But I was in too deep to care. I needed to redeem my humble beginnings, to feel like I was somebody. And since I wasn't anybody yet, it seemed like most ethical bets were off.

I understood Prince Machiavelli. You have to want something really badly before the Prince becomes your pal. It's easy to be all virtuous when you've never cared too much about something, but just try craving something *really* passionately if you want your dark side revealed to you. Craving utterly ruins ethics. Craving inverts the entire world; the ends justify whatever means you use and only an idiot thinks they don't. I hated who I became on that job, though I wasn't the biggest schmuck by a long shot.

The Passions

WE ASPIRE BECAUSE PASSION gives meaning to our lives. *"Un homme sans passion et desires cesserait d'etre un homme,"* wrote von Holbach, a philosopher of the French Enlightenment. A man without passions or desires would cease to be a man. Not being wantons, our need for physical survival runs alongside a parallel craving for quality of life, ego fulfillment, distinction, transcendence, and meaning. No one has written more trenchantly about the passions than Erich Fromm. He tells us that passion is what transforms human beings from "things" to "heroes," making us agents instead of "nature's playthings." Passion is what drove Jared Miller from his meaningless, alcoholic, bachelor life to helping women start their own businesses in Rwanda. Passion is also what prompted Burton Pugach—the famed Othello who had lye thrown in his fiancée's face—to hire a hit man to teach her a lesson (she later became his blind wife). "The truth is that all human passions, both the 'good' and the 'evil' can be understood only as a person's attempt to make sense of his life and transcend banal, merely life-sustaining existence," Fromm explains, paradoxically.

We can't always know where passion will take us. Because we have only one life to live, to paraphrase Milan Kundera, we cannot conduct experiments to test whether to follow this passion or that one. In our efforts to counter what the novelist called the unbearable lightness of being (the specter of our own insignificance), each of us is forced to follow his or her passions in an experiment that Kundera suggests is "running on autopilot." This is further confused by the opposing modes of passion—the so-called life instinct and death instinct—that animate us. While the life instinct may be more constructive, things stemming from the death instinct can sometimes provide as much of an answer to the problem of human existence as the former, Fromm reports. "Life turning against itself in the striving to make sense of it," he writes, fuels our destructive tendencies and nourishes the roots of evil.

Freud was the first to recognize where the "death instinct" came from, of course, and why, to counteract it, we adapted by growing such an enormous frontal cortex, where higher reasoning and moral perception take place. By the 1920s, Freud had already revised his earlier theory centered around the sexual drive to one in which the passion to destroy, or death instinct, was considered equal in strength to the passion to love, or life instinct. With self-consciousness came the human cri de coeur, existential dread, and the rest of our unique malaises. "Man cannot live as nothing but an object, as dice thrown out of a cup," Fromm warned. "He suffers severely when he is reduced to the level of a feeding or propagating machine, even if he has all the security he wants. Man seeks for drama and excitement; when he cannot get satisfaction on a higher level, he creates for himself the drama of destruction."

Aside from lemmings, few animals have a death instinct—wantons are too self-preserving. We, on the other hand, often act according to our destructive passions, risking self-interest, fortune, freedom—even our lives—in the pursuit of love, truth, and integrity, in our struggle to *signify*. This seizability by passion is our human cross to bear. We're born with a perverse streak, an incorrigible need to betray our own standards. Just as we aspire to greatness, we long for our own lower depths as well. We need to trespass our own standards sometimes, to fall, behave badly, and be inconsistent. The doubleness of our passions requires a mix of darkness and light to make a happy whole. A chink of breathing room is required between who we really are and who we'd be if we were perfect. This helps to explain why Oprah continues to regain the weight and Obama may not want to quit the butts for good. While our black-or-white perfectionism wants to stamp out every darkness and vice, this intolerance has more to do with narcissism, power, fear, and control than it does with human goodness.

This is a lesson I learned the hard way. I used to have a perfection complex. I wanted military precision and the wherewithal to rule my own life. A neurotic amount of energy was invested into cleaning up my act, stopping bad habits, and flagellating myself. I believed that, through such pious self-loathing I would achieve some squeaky-clean version of integrity, where shame disappeared and I would finally become my own master. This struggle inside me rarely subsided. There was always something more to give up, another weakness to muzzle myself against, another kink in my character—cigarettes, backbiting, hamburgers, TV, booze, caffeine, fried food—that appeared to stand between me and my ideal doppelgänger. This crusade to sanitize my own checkered nature was doomed, though. Sooner or later—mostly sooner—my dream self would take the plunge into vice, compelled by some down-pulling, mischievous voice that *needed* that falling sense in order to feel completely alive. No amount of self-mockery helped. Something in me needed to be bad sometimes in order to feel really good. Though I aimed for temperance, order, and wisdom, the urge toward delinquency and wickedness could not be ignored as important—if impious, aspects of living.

Much has been written about the psychological shadow, the hiding place for our darker instincts. But not enough has been explained regarding the positive function of vice in our lives, and how important it is for us to maintain some internal forbidden zone where we can betray ourselves now and then. Falling appears to be what matters. The urge to throw ourselves into the shadowy depths may well be a mental check on vanity, grandiosity, and perfectionism. Without a whiff of forbidden fruit, the personality starts to mildew, shut away in its too-good cage. Vice keeps a moral window ajar and lets in the darkness to keep us authentic. Otherwise life becomes a virtuous pose, a tepid ethical Girl Scout ego trip without the cookies.

Are there parts of your shadow you don't accept? Secret inclinations you tend to reject in order to act like a soi-disant saint? What dark desires have you kept hostage down in your clandestine passion bunker? Personally, I'm a closet smoker. Since lighting up my first cigarette at twelve, the year we pulled out of Vietnam, I've remained an intractable, semisecret butthead, flirting with this filthy compulsion—quitting, starting, stopping again for years at a time. I swear that I will stop for good (I'm in one of those moments now, God help me) but always have returned—with an odd combination of pleasure, relief, and shame—to a stinking habit I know to be deadly. I'm addicted, of course, and I'm spineless, too, but that doesn't really explain the obsession. The magnetic attraction of vice, I think, has more to do with keeping a shadowy corner of oneself, *for oneself,* in the too-bright, too-conscious, too-good room of life in our health-obsessed culture. We all need to blow off virtue sometimes, to flip the bird at self-improvement. The French refer to this abandon as *je m'enfoutisme,* the brave art of not giving a damn. That's the secret reason why people smoke, have affairs, bungee jump, drink too much, and require more-than-occasional excess; why, no matter how right we are, sometimes we all need to be slightly wrong too, refusing to cut off that one last wart. Vice reminds us that we'll never be perfect and *that's a good thing.* Life isn't some filthy mess to be cleaned up, all spic-and-span—like Mary Hartman, the sitcom heroine, scrubbing madly at her kitchen floor till she can see her miserable reflection in the linoleum. We're more complex creatures than puritans would have us believe and our passions, to qualify as such, sometimes need not make a lick of sense.

Vice in moderation humanizes—even improves—character. Why else do we feel most intimate with others during down-and-dirty interludes when our superegos are checked at the door and our ids are having all the fun? Think about the people you love and ask yourself if it isn't their so-called weaknesses that draw them closest to you somehow, in spite of how much you respect their strengths. Ask yourself whether intimacy, in fact, might not be forged in these very falling-down places, where people we care about stumble and fall, and never manage to stand up completely—just like us. Would you rather be stuck on a desert island with a hell-raising pagan or the snippy-mouthed Church Lady from *Saturday Night Live*—if you're honest? My point exactly.

My nonconformist mother used to say this in her own way. "Rules were made to be broken," Ida liked to remind me when I was being too hard on myself. She knew that my life was one long attempt to prove her wrong, to captain my own wobbly ship. Till one day, my mother finally called my bluff. Decades after I'd moved out of her house, she found me in the garage, smoking one of her unfiltered Pall Malls during some tormented, virtuous period. I'll never forget the delighted look on her face, or how my mother smirked as she lit one herself and sat next to me on the washing machine. Looking back at the two of us there, I realize that this was among our most intimate moments; she died a few years later. Though I struggled to hide my weakness from her, my mother knew it better than anyone. For a long time, we sat there smoking without a word, till finally she stubbed hers out and stood to leave me to myself. Before she went, my mother turned and asked me what I was really so afraid of.

I told her that I didn't know.

"Being human?"

Vice can coexist with wisdom. I've met some Zen masters who are the biggest rascals you've ever met in your life. I think of John Daido Loori, the resident teacher at the Zen Mountain Monastery in Mount Tremper, New York. I used to meditate at the monastery on Sunday mornings when I was pretending to be a monk in a cabin in upstate New York without a car one hideous summer. Daido Loori would come in, all stately and fierce in his black robes, surrounded by ritual bowers and scrapers, deliver his dharma talk about nothingness being somethingness, then speed away from the hall after breakfast in a golf cart, sucking on a Benson and Hedges, a sailor's tattoo on his forearm from when he served in the U.S. Navy. I've known a lot of pretty fine teachers and not a single one has been lily white.

By remembering that our life-thwarting passions serve the same existential function as our life-enhancing ones, we free ourselves of puritan judgment and accept our human need for mischief. By indulging the wayward parts of ourselves, we actually enhance vitality. Passion must contain risk. And risk can cut both ways.

FREEDOM

Freedom may be the greatest passion of all, from political freedom to freedom of consciousness. Every person who sees a therapist is seeking freedom of some kind, surcease from some agony. Every person who goes to a church or temple seeks freedom from the mundane and the tawdry. Liberation, as defined by Buddhists, is the awareness of space outside the mind-cage. We can be free in prison cells; we can also be free on our own deathbeds if we've done the spiritual prep work. We can be free, or free-ish, almost anywhere. Or we can feel imprisoned. "Wherever a man is against his will, that is to him a prison," Epictetus tells us. A lot of people feel trapped in their own lives.

Individuals are also liberated in places and ways we might not expect. I interviewed a Sudanese man named Francis Bok who'd been kidnapped as a seven-year-old boy and came to write a book called *Escape from Slavery*. It may surprise you to learn that there are several hundred million people living as slaves in the world today. One morning in 1986, Francis was sitting in a dusty marketplace near his family's farm in the hinterlands of eastern Sudan. He was there with his sisters selling produce from the family's homestead, among the most fertile in the valley. As the strongest son of eight, Francis was his father's favorite, the boy he called *muycharko*—a Dinka word meaning "twelve men"—the child his father had chosen to replace him as head of the family after he died. The children were spread out on a crimson blanket under their lean-to of burlap and sticks, laughing, surrounded by their wares.

All of a sudden, bedlam broke out. Francis heard gunfire and galloping horses, crowds scattering in all directions as a band of black-turbaned marauders stormed into the marketplace. These were the dreaded *juur*, members of the Arab tribes to the north who'd sworn genocide against southern black Christians like Francis and his family. As Francis watched in terror, his five-year-old sister hiding behind him, these *juur* began to hack down people in the marketplace. Francis's neighbor, a girl of eight, was shot through the head for no reason; when her sister became hysterical and refused to leave the girl's dead body, she had her leg hacked off at the hip. Women and babies were bayoneted and left to writhe to their death in the dirt. The terrified boy herded his sisters behind him. Before they could escape, a man was there on horseback, towering over him, pointing a gun at Francis's head, and ordering the boy into the saddle behind him. Then the horse was galloping out past the road to Francis's farm and into the desert highway leading toward Khartoum.

Fourteen hours later, Francis and his kidnapper, Giemma Abdullah, arrived at Giemma's farm, where Francis was shackled, locked in a pigsty, and told that he was now *abeed*—a slave—who would live and eat with the animals. If Francis disobeyed in any way, or tried to escape, Giemma assured him that he would be killed. For no reason whatsoever, Giemma's wife pulled Francis into the kitchen one morning, put a pistol to his head, and with an evil smile said, "I would blow your brains out this very minute if I could." Giemma's children were invited to beat Francis with rocks and sticks as a game. "I wondered why no one was helping me," Francis told me. "People just stood there and watched. Why would they do that to me? I was only seven years old." Night after night in his pigsty, gazing up through a hole in the roof, Francis began to plot and replot his escape from Giemma's farm. "Better not to live," he decided, "than to live as a slave."

After ten years of slavery, Francis did manage to escape to freedom. When we spoke in his small apartment outside Boston (he'd been rescued and helped to immigrate by an antislavery group in Washington, D.C.), he explained how the need for freedom had kept him alive.

"I reached the point inside of myself that I didn't care what would happen to me," he tells me. "I didn't care if I lived or died. I only knew that I must try to escape."

He looks like a Giacometti sculpture dipped and polished in blue-black ink, his body, at six feet seven inches, impossibly thin, severely chiseled, astoundingly odd in its elongation. The little apartment, with its thrift store furniture, Lakers basketball posters, and color TV, could belong to any college student (Francis is taking courses at a nearby university). This backdrop seems a universe away from the fields where he and his brother grew up playing *alweth* (hide-and-seek) near their village of Gourion.

Ten years after his abduction, following a number of close calls, the seventeen-year-old was finally able to slip off Giemma Abdullah's farm while herding cattle, hitched a ride to a local town, and then—after several detours—found his way to Khartoum, where he was arrested on suspicion of illegal activity and finally shipped to Cairo. After four months in Egypt, Francis's case was taken up by a human rights group, and he was granted asylum in the United States, where a foster family supported him long enough for Francis to afford the small apartment where he and I are now sitting.

"What kept you going?" I wonder.

"I am a Christian," Francis says, as if that explained everything. "I can tell you this," he adds in a voice so low I can hardly hear him. "No matter what happens, I try to take it soft."

"What do you mean by soft?"

"I have learned that it does not matter how much you are beaten or how much you are despised," he says, ignoring my question. "There is one thing that they can never take from you."

"What?"

He leans forward, earnestly. "They can never steal your idea of who you are. They can never take control of your mind. They can never take away your self-love."

It's easy to see him behind a pulpit.

"They cannot take away my forgiveness. They can never silence my heart. No matter what has happened, I see myself as a full person."

I find this astonishing. The majority of people I know have not endured a fraction of Francis's losses, and still do not see themselves as full people. "How is that possible?" I ask, hoping not to sound rude.

"If you want to live, you must fight for your freedom." Francis clasps his hands together. As a Christian, Francis believes in mercy but is dedicated to the struggle for justice, too. Today, he travels the world telling people about slavery. "When you abandon yourself, you lose," he says. "If you are alive in this world, you must fight. But never with a sword. My people are using machine guns to shoot the Arabs who are slaughtering us. They believe that is the way to freedom, but it is not."

"What about anger?"

He reaches for a paperback book on the coffee table. It is Dickens's *A Tale of Two Cities*. Francis turns to the first page. "It was the best of times, it was the worst of times," he reads, picking his way through the English letters. "This is what my life has been like," he says, smiling. "The best and the worst."

"This is the best part?"

"I have been given a second chance."

"You forgave Giemma?"

Francis closes the book and puts it down. Then he looks me straight in the eye and echoes the Buddha's Fire Sermon nearly word for word.

"No one can move forward in hatred," he says.

"But how do you *feel*, Francis?"

"Dignity does not come from bloodshed. There must be a way—you must find it—to love. There is no other way. Otherwise—"

"What?"

"Otherwise," Francis looks into my eyes, "I am just like Giemma."

How Ought I to Live?

Part Five

[PURITY/SACREDNESS]

There is a power at the center of our being, at the
heart of all things living. But only in man does
it assume a spiritual character. And only through
spirit does life continue by decision.

—TERRENCE DES PRES

The Holy Question

HOW OUGHT I TO LIVE? One day in Cape Town, South Africa, an exapartheid honcho named Eugene de Kock made a surprising request to his captors at the prison where he was serving a life sentence. One of the more notoriously vicious murderers in the apartheid regime, de Kock had undergone some process of extreme contrition, and wanted to personally apologize to the widows of his victims. De Kock asked that the meeting be held in private. To everyone's surprise, the widows' lawyer agreed, and one morning in 1997, Pearl Faku and Doreen Mgoduka arrived at the prison to meet the man who had killed their husbands.

De Kock expressed his excruciating shame. "I was raised to think of you as animals," he told the women before breaking down in uncontrollable sobs. A few days later, the women described the meeting to a psychologist. They said that de Kock, "a monster of mythic repute," astonished them by communicating how deeply he regretted what he had done, as well as the pain he'd caused their families. The women found themselves unexpectedly elevated by the spectacle of his true remorse.

"I was profoundly touched by him," Mrs. Faku told the psychologist. Then she reported doing something that shocked de Kock and herself. She reached out and took his hand. It was his trigger hand, he told her in tears, the hand he'd used to kill so many black people. "I was so moved by his pain," Mrs. Faku said. "I related to him in the only way one does in such circumstances. I touched his hand." Something profound had taken place. "If showing compassion to our enemies is something that our bodies recoil from," asked Mrs. Mgoduka, "what should our attitude be to their cries for mercy? The cries that tell us that their hearts are breaking and that they are willing to renounce their past and their role in it?"

How can we forgive unforgivable things?

"I hope that when he sees our tears, he knows that they are not only tears for our husbands, but tears for him as well," the widow said. "I would like to hold him by the hand, and show him that there is a future, and that he can still change." Hard as the memory of having touched him was, the experience made her realize something she was not prepared for, she told the psychologist. "I learned that good and evil exist in all our lives, and that evil, like good, is always a possibility. And that is what frightened me."

This wasn't saintly; it was, however, wise beyond most of our reach. "You must be strong to forgive," one Holocaust survivor put it. "Forgiveness is not about condoning or excusing. Forgiveness has nothing to do with justice. Forgiving is a selfish act to free yourself from being controlled by your past." In ordinary life, fear, pain, and anger herd us back and forth between shifting camps of good and evil. In sacredness, a third response takes place. When we face ourselves in our enemies, the dualistic mind is turned around—the Greeks called this *metanoia*—allowing us to countenance human complexity without protection. The widows learned this that day in prison with de Kock. Weeping when they saw his tears, they stepped across an abyss of grief and touched, for a moment, sacredness.

There's a wonderful story from the *Iliad* about this. Near the end of the Trojan War, Achilles, the famous warrior, decides to pull his troops out of the conflict. In the course of the ensuing muddle, his beloved friend Patroclus is killed by the Trojan prince, Hector. Achilles goes mad with grief, rage, and revenge, murders Hector, mutilates his corpse, and refuses to give the body back to the family for burial. One night, Hector's father, Priam, king of Troy, puts on a disguise and slips into the Greek camp incognito.

Priam makes his way to Achilles's tent to ask for the body of his son. Seeing the old man, Achilles thinks of his own father and starts to weep. At that moment, Priam looks at the man who has murdered so many of his sons and he, too, starts to weep, "and the sound of their weeping filled the house." The Greeks believed that weeping together created a bond between people. They believed that sharing grief dissolved the paper-thin boundary between the guilty and the innocent, revealing the truth that encompasses both. Achilles then took the body of Hector and handed it to Priam very tenderly. And in that moment of compassion, the two men looked at one another and saw each other as divine.

This is the goodness we're capable of when we transcend naïveté and self-consecration, tribalism and *lex talionis*. It's the sacred dimension afforded to us by the moral organ itself, which is programmed for divine connection that may have nothing to do with religion. Aware of our clay feet, we reach upward. This vertical movement is divine with or without a particular God. Our passion for enlargement comes through self-forgetting, at least temporarily. Man's need for transcendence, typically imposed on God, may in fact be "god" in a purely symbolic sense of "not-self." This yearning for *meta*-physical life is the reason for religious programming in our brain. The religious impulse strengthens and extends the cohesion provided by our moral systems. Without a religious bent of mind, scientists tell us, we'd still be just small bands roving around with no greater roof to congregate under, spiritually speaking. Instead, we come equipped with a mechanism for the suppression of self in order to connect to a larger Self. Studies of religious experience show that people have decreased activity in the brain areas that maintain maps of the self's boundaries and position, like Jill Bolte Taylor crammed in that bathtub. We don't merge with the universe; we remember the universe. We synchronize with those around us. Studies of ritual, particularly those involving the sort of synchronized movements common in religious rites, indicate that such rituals serve to bind participants together in ecstatic states of union.

We also bind together in love. "Except as we have loved, / All news arrives as from a distant land," Mary Oliver writes in her poem "Beyond the Snow Belt." We take love to be our highest standard, the purity of human embrace. We do this in groups, but more intensely in couples, where we practice the day-to-day art of kindness (and on bad days, decency). We can only know what we have loved, and the sense of this—that without the act of opening, we know nothing— is transcendent and true. At its heart, love is very simple. We need only switch our focus from self to other and become grateful for each other's existence. Love becomes a path to the sacred, something pure in a sometimes demoralized world. "Love is rejoicing over the existence of the beloved one," begins a gorgeous description that I won't resist quoting in full:

> Love is gratitude. It is thankfulness for the existence of the beloved; it is the happy acceptance of everything that he gives without the jealous feeling that the self ought to be able to do as much; it is gratitude that does not seek equality; it is wonder over the other's gift of himself in companionship. Love is reverence: it keeps its distance even as it draws near; it does not seek to absorb the other in the self or want to be absorbed by it; it rejoices in the otherness of the

other; it desires the beloved to be what he is and does not seek to refashion him into a replica of the self or to make him a means to the self's advancement. As reverence, love is and seeks knowledge of the other, not by way of curiosity nor for the sake of gaining power but in rejoicing and in wonder. In all such love there is an element of that "holy fear" which is not a form of flight but rather deep respect for the otherness of the beloved and the profound unwillingness to violate his integrity. Love is loyalty; it is the willingness to let the self be destroyed rather than that the other cease to be; it is the commitment of the self by self-binding will to make the other great.

Those are pretty tall marching orders, but what could be worthier of doing? What could be more wise?

Zoroastrians believe that gravity, the force drawing planets together in space, is love itself. John Dewey, of library fame, came to an oddly similar conclusion. The father of the Dewey decimal system was apparently a closet mystic: "The spiritual life [gets] its surest and most ample guarantees when it is learned that the laws and conditions of righteousness are implicated in the working processes of the universe; when it is found that man in his conscious struggles, in his doubts, temptations and defeats, in his aspirations and successes, is moved on and buoyed up by the forces which have developed nature." When we look at ourselves this way, as upcroppings of nature obeying harmonious laws, something beams inside the brain. Our moral sense is sharpened and heightened, elevated by something greater.

"It is with the heart that one sees rightly; what is essential is invisible to the eye," Saint-Exupery believed. Compassion's path is steep but rewarding. Observers of Mother Teresa were sometimes puzzled by the enigma of the nun's compassion. One of the things that most astonished them was this complex woman's ability to give and receive joy while holding a hopelessly ill infant. How could she bear the anguish of so many confrontations with sickness and death? she was often asked. Mother Teresa spoke of gratitude in being able to fulfill her soul's potential. She was fond of saying that every suffering body she touched was "Christ in his distressing disguise." There is nothing more mysterious and rare than agape: unconditional devotion. When we meet people capable of such vast, impersonal love, we too feel enlarged and drawn to service.

We are told by Buddhist teachers, and I believe it, that "the natural radiance of mind is its innate wakefulness." We are born to be beamed up, Scotty. It is the open, knowing nature of the mind itself that seeks this larger, deeper, higher connection. The Tibetan word for radiance also means "able to know." We realize, as humans, that our mandate is unique and awesome: to know ourselves as parts of a vast cosmos we do not control, whose magnificence we can conceptualize, then mirror in the imagination with feelings of cosmic unity. Monkeys stare at the moon but only we have Rumi. Only we have mystery and sacredness, the long view, the horizon that seems to end with us, then passes through us to the next sentient being. As I was finishing this book, an article appeared profiling V. Ramachandran, the neurologist, in which the maverick thinker posits how it is that self-awareness may have been born in us in the first place. Mirror neurons, explained Ramachandran, give us what's called allocentric perspective, the ability to see from someone else's shoes, rather than our usual egocentric view. Ramachandran has a theory that sometime in human evolution, *these mirror neurons turned back on us,* allowing us to be aware of ourselves. Think about this. A neuron in your brain has turned back on the brain itself, like one of those solar disks spinning out in the desert, to reveal an animal *to* itself for the first time in earth's history. Without this, we would not have awe. We would not know how tiny we really are in a galaxy we have photographed. It is crucial to have a window *onto* that view, to brighten life when it gets confusing, and remind us that—painful as existence can sometimes be—we really are a miracle.

All of it is miraculous. Still, our potential for growth scares the hell out of us. "Our deepest fear is not that we are inadequate, but that we are powerful beyond measure," Nelson Mandela said after being released from prison. "It is our light, not our darkness, that most frightens us." We take comfort in the ordinary because, though magnificent, we are tiny, too, both contractualists and hive players. Not tiny, infinitesimal. This is the cosmic joke, after all: having hardware that can measure our own diminution, predict and study our own extinction, sift through the ashes of what we become and discover that we're made from stardust. This is astonishing, which is why we mostly try not to think about it. Imagine if we really were self-aware, how mind-blowing that would be! Imagine if we did not fear our own limits, what beauty and wisdom we could engender, what genius? Merely considering this opens a mental window. That is the function of sacredness in our lives. The holy question cannot make us divine, but it can give us the dream of wings. The sacred sense tells us that *this*—the superficial layer of existence—isn't the entire picture; that each of our lives is defined by our dreams, and how we choose to transcend our limits.

Without holiness—the potential for it—we could not survive. Human life is far too brutal. Without the practice of sacredness in our lives, we could never withstand the nightmarish parts, the sorrows, losses, injustice, betrayals, apathy, and horror. The physical body might persevere, but the spirit would die in its chrysalis with its eye closed against the divine. Deprived of an essential connection—the feeling that though we die, we matter—hope perishes and with it the aspiration to goodness. Honor slumps into complacency; evolution gives way to regret. We lose the magic and ourselves when the world is stripped of its sacred dimension. We can't perceive radiance when we're squinting. *Aux yeux ouverts*, with open eyes, the French call seeing the world in all its glory. Atheist or true believer, we can sacramentalize our lives by waking to wonder, the now-and-never-again-for-all-time-ness of things, and bring this tenderness to other people.

We must keep our eye on the grandeur of things—not in a grandiose way, but as a reality check. Otherwise, we find ourselves shrinking. That's all too common a situation in our demystified world. And we wonder why depression rates are rising. Depression is more than a chemical condition. Mircea Eliade, the great historian of sacred traditions, captured our situation prophetically: "The modern West is the first culture in human history that has managed to strip time and space of all sacredness and to produce a fully practical, efficient, and profane world," with its material focus, mass consumption, individualist ethos, and reliance on science as the bottom line. We err too far on the side of left-brain order and lose a measure of right-brain enchantment. In a materialistic culture, as a friend used to say, we have no transcendental context for our suffering.

Matthew Fox, a former Catholic priest who was silenced by the Vatican for calling the church a dysfunctional patriarchy—which it is—put it to me this way: "We've been Novocained to death by . . . all our addictions, from entertainment to workaholism to drinking and drugging. It covers up our capacity for awe. For passion and deep feeling. It sets us up for superficial experience." Then Fox quoted another religious man, the Jewish philosopher Abraham Joshua Heschel, who surmised that modern man is "shocked by the weakness of our awe, but also by the weakness of our shock." When we shut down the sacred, we shut down wisdom. Without a feeling for the sublime, disgust robs us of luster, and the hope of making a better world.

It's interesting to note that in ages past, good and evil were mixed up with sacred and profane in very different ways than they are today. Among the Australian Aborigines, for example, religion wasn't about God—or any deity—but about the distinction between sacred and profane. The sacred could be good or evil, and the profane could be either as well. This is the view that I subscribe to. Otherwise, we're subjected to man-made rules pretending to do the work of God and punishing people for being human. Wisdom knows that sacredness exists in the lowliest places (compassion among prisoners and prostitutes) and that profanity proliferates at the heart of what we consider sacrosanct (priests who rape). Redefining sacredness and profanity allows us to behold our world *aux yeux ouverts*, widening the ethical shutter, seeing things for what they are, not being fooled by facades of goodness or greatness. Hitler's favorite moviemaker, Leni Riefenstahl, made Nazism look heavenly in her beautiful 1936 film *Olympia*. The surface is sublime and stirring, the underside a nightmare. That's the problem with the sublime. By definition the sublime involves great heights. And what we look up to has the power to dominate us.

The desire for purity creates the need for sin, of course, and for systems that punish moral offense. But what is sin, we ask ourselves? Do we sin by being born, rendering ourselves forever culpable? Do we sin when we break with tradition, marry outside our faith, eat meat and dairy from the same plate, have more than one wife or a same-sex partner? Is sin, like justice, a local, culture-bound concept, or is there an objective basis for judging sinfulness? There are moralists who believe that sin lies in human contradiction itself. "The whole meaning of sin is the humiliating bondage of the higher to the lower," wrote geologist Joseph Le Conte, sounding like poor tormented Cotton Mather peeing behind that tree. But why so humiliating, guys? Galling, frustrating, no walk in the park? Okay. Confounding, absurd, ridiculous sometimes? Of course. But humiliating? Not so much. To be humiliated over simply being human is grandiose. Fear of our so-called lower nature perverts morality into moralism, slicing, chopping, and scalloping the world into too many opposing pieces that aren't actually disconnected. I prefer the original meaning of sin: to miss the mark. There's no splitting of the world in this view; life becomes a case-by-case judgment call to do the best we can for the greater good. We aim to hit the mark in our lives, but the mark is not in a fixed position. Not only that, but the struggle to hit the mark has virtue and goodness in itself, and is inseparable from self-realization. In his short book *Intentions,* Oscar Wilde, no stranger to bad behavior, argues that "What is termed Sin is an essential element of progress," and that "[without] it, the world would stagnate, or grow old, or become colourless." "By its curiosity, sin increases the experience of the race," Wilde wrote. "Through its intensified assertion of individualism, it saves us from monotony of type. In its rejection of the current notions about morality, it is one with the higher ethics." Our job is to know the difference between sinning well and sinning badly.

The pragmatic question is: How? Mindfulness is an excellent tool for cultivating openheartedness and wisdom. Becoming more mindful in one's own life is like becoming your own chief of staff. The right hand knows what the slacker in the left hemisphere is planning before it's too late. Attention is being paid. If we want something done, mindfully speaking, we know which guy to turn to. Mindfulness is the power that harnesses wisdom. As the classic Buddhist teaching goes:

Mind is the forerunner of all things.
If one speaks or acts with an impure mind
Suffering follows, like the wheel that follows the foot of the ox.

Mind is the forerunner of all things.
If one speaks or acts with a pure mind
Happiness follows, like the shadow that never leaves.

Without mindfulness, we lose track of thoughts and intentions; we abandon ourselves to confusion and stumbling. When we're paying attention, cause-and-effect connections become more apparent. When our actions are motivated by kindness, generosity, wisdom, and love, we can't help noticing how much better we feel. When anger, greed, or delusion drives us, the mayhem that follows is hard to miss. When we assemble the reins of the body, take our mental seat, and center ourselves in good intention—the Buddha called it "right intention"—the horses of mind can be made to gallop together rather than foaming at the mouth and breaking their necks. We learn to settle into the seat that's made just for us—our unique personal way of seeing—and welcome the impartial spectator who knows he's not impartial but observes our antics with amusement, generosity, patience, and wit. Mindfulness relies on balance, just as wisdom does. Both bring happiness into our lives. It was Colette who said that being happy is a way of being wise. While I assume that she didn't meditate, the promiscuous novelist did have access to her own inner seat, the center of her mental carriage. The formidable writer could hunker down deep in her wisdom seat even as she passed through hell, with a boy toy in her bed at home, and a pug dog snoring in her lap.

There are techniques for doing this, using neuroplasticity to wake ourselves up, increasing gamma activity in our brains (as meditation and contemplative practices have been shown to do) and lowering heartache. These tools are salvific and widely available. All of them share a common element: single-pointedness. When we still the mind enough to focus on one object—the breath, a candle, a prayer, a wall—we quiet down enough to acquaint ourselves with our mental playing field. This is a difficult but rewarding process that changes our inner experience. Nothing is separate, we begin to realize. The mind's confabulations become apparent; we notice that everything outside this moment, in this room, on this bus, or wherever we are, is only happening inside our minds. From where we're sitting, we are actually making up the world, quite often missing out on what is right in front of our noses. So we learn to sit, or learn to breathe; we learn to tolerate ourselves, learn to do one thing at a time, and find ourselves improved by this patience. The results of mindfulness happen now. No imagination or faith is required.

We find sacredness in everyday things. We're reminded of the Delphic oracle's advice to know ourselves, first and foremost. An innocence is returned to us by sitting, fully, inside our own skins, with the lights on, watching, wondering, and waiting for gaps in our thoughts to leave us in peace. Mindful moments may be rare, but once you have had them you don't want to stop. Quotidian life gets much more interesting. All of a sudden we're *in the building*. The view is exceedingly strange and alive.

There's sacredness in existence itself. "Human-heartedness," religious writer Karen Armstrong calls it. Self-awareness increases other-awareness. The alternative is what we have now: ethical live-stock without a head, wondering why it can't see straight. There are too many ways to kill one another; the law of averages is now against us. Beyond laws of probabilities, we find the sacred, however; possi-bilities beyond what we know and the human-heartedness to get us there. This process must grow with conviction now. We must not, as Armstrong told an audience recently, confine compassion to our own group. "You must have concern for everybody," Armstrong said. She cited God's warning to mankind in the Koran. "We formed you into tribes and nations so you may *know* one another," she said. This would be a victory for our species as a whole: a way of dis-pelling our ignorance.

It's natural, if you're alive, to be puzzled; life is complex and changeable. The sacred and the profane dance together. A penniless woman steals a blue coat. She does it because she loves her son. She believes that rules are made to be broken; she's right in a sense, but not completely. She loves a man who isn't hers. She waits to see him every Tuesday night, wearing her only pair of high heels, because she cannot stop herself—nor can he, with his crippled wife and crippling despair. She makes him happy; their love is sacred, every week at the Tropicana Motel. My mother was reaching, I see that now, for love and for our satisfaction, for a moment of feeling like she was good, to someone, for something, at least for a while. All of us are reaching.

"Set your heart on doing good," the Buddha taught. "Do it over and over again, and you will be filled with joy. A fool is happy until his mischief turns against him. And a good man may suffer until his goodness flowers."

Tests, Games, and Challenges

1. There are lots of reasons to love Ben Franklin—the key, the hairdo, the hundred-dollar bill—but Franklin was also the most self-consciously virtuous of our founding fathers. In 1726, at the age of twenty, Franklin developed a plan for monitoring his future conduct while on a transatlantic trip from London back to Philadelphia. The plan, which Franklin followed with unwavering diligence to his death, was a list of thirteen virtues with brief instructions for each one. At the end of his life, Franklin attributed most of his happiness to following this list:

- Temperance: Eat not to dullness; drink not to elevation.
- Silence: Speak not but what may benefit others or yourself; avoid trifling conversation.
- Order: Let all your things have their places; let each part of your business have its time.
- Resolution: Resolve to perform what you ought; perform without fail what you resolve.

- Frugality: Make no expense but to do good to others or yourself; i.e., waste nothing.
- Industry: Lose no time; be always employed in something useful; cut off all unnecessary actions.
- Sincerity: Use no hurtful deceit; think innocently and justly, and, if you speak, speak accordingly.
- Justice: Wrong none by doing injuries, or omitting the benefits that are your duty.
- Moderation: Avoid extremes; forbear resenting injuries so much as you think they deserve.
- Cleanliness: Tolerate no uncleanliness in body, clothes, or habitation.
- Tranquility: Be not disturbed at trifles, or at accidents common or unavoidable.
- Chastity: Rarely use venery but for health or offspring, never to dullness, weakness, or the injury of your own or another's peace or reputation.
- Humility: Imitate Jesus and Socrates.

Franklin would commit to one virtue a week, so that after thirteen weeks he had completed the list. Then he would begin again (he could do four cycles a year). Get yourself a notebook and give this a try.

2. How egotistical are you? Asking people to examine their egos is like telling fish to focus their eyes on water. Because we believe that we *are* our egos, we have difficulty separating selfishness from having a self. But these are two different things. For an ego check, visit http://www.quiztron.com/tests/egotistical_quiz 44174.htm.

3. How altruistic are you? Where does your generosity fall on the spectrum of possibilities rising from Machiavelli to Gandhi?

How much does it take to make you generous? Try taking the Altruism Test at http://www.quizmoz.com/quizzes/Personalilty Tests/a/Are-You-Altruistic.asp.

4. Speaking of Machiavelli, if you don't know what a jerk you can be, whether beneath the surface you're a cutthroat or a pussy-cat, try being appalled by the Machiavelli personality test at http://www.salon.com/books/it/1999/09/13/machtest/.

5. Where do you locate your center of power? Within yourself or outside your control? This is a critical question for everyone. If you want to know where your plug is located, have a look at the Internal/External Locus of Control Test at http://www.psych .uncc.edu/pagoolka/LC.html.

6. Everybody's a character. "Character" comes from the Greek word for "etching," and it's true that we're all composite portraits. But we also share certain general human traits and character types that reveal themselves in an ethical crisis. For a look at your character type, check out http://www.graphic insight.co.za/games.htm.

7. What about hostility? Are you quick to anger, or cucumber cool? Reasonable or a ticking time bomb? Or both on the same day? Gauge yourself using the Hostility Test: http://www .queendom.com/tests/access_page/index.htm?idRegTest=1124.

8. Is all fair in love and war? Do you believe that different rules apply when Cupid's arrow is in your behind? A fool in love is a fool indeed, right? Have a look-see at the Love and Ethics Puzzle: http://www.thoughtware.com.au/philosophy/ puzzles/puzzle1.html.

9. What's your basic philosophical stance? Is man beholden to other men first? Or do you believe that chips fall where they may? Do accidents exist? Or is there a master plan to which we are merely obedient? Probe and question at http://www.select smart.com/PHILOSOPHY/.

10. The Jung Personality Type Test is sure to leave you feeling larger than life. Freud's disciple was big on dreams, myths, and symbols, and you might be, too, if you get with the archetypal program. http://www.humanmetrics.com/cgi-win/JTypes2.asp.

11. How logical are you? Can you think your way through a complex dilemma, and actually make the thinking stick? Or do emotions cancel out reasoning more often than you would like? Figure out where your fault lines are at http://www.quibblo.com/quiz/2KWN0OO/How-logical-are-you.

12. If you still haven't figured it out after that, try another logic game that approaches the same problem from the other direction: http://blogthings.com/howlogicalareyouquiz/.

13. And how rational are you? Reason is not the same as logic—logic is reason at its source, without some of the cultural overlay. Our rationalizing tool goes from sharp to dull, depending on the time of day. Where do you fall in the line of unreason? http://www.okcupid.com/tests/take?testid= 16529184738850296340.

14. During the Middle Ages the body was believed to be ruled by four fluids, or "humours," that ran through our physical organism. An imbalance in these humours led to a dominance of different personality traits. Take this test to find out which of

the four humours dominates your personality: http://quizilla
.teennick.com/quizzes/1006214/which-of-the-humours-
are-you.

15. Nobody is completely honest—nor are people quite as *dishonest* as we might believe. How honest are you? Find out at
http://blogthings.com/howhonestareyouquiz/.

Notes

Introduction

6   **Moral foundations theory**: Jonathan Haidt, MoralFoundations.org (homepage).

10   **"Dalai Lama neurons"**: V. Ramachandran, "Mirror Neurons and the Brain in a Vat," *Edge*, January 10, 2006, available at http://www.edge.org.

10   **"expanding the circle"**: P. Singer, "The Drowning Child and the Expanding Circle," *New Internationalist*, April 1997 (online).

11   **"increasingly important subcontractors"**: Lance Morrow, *Evil: An Investigation*, Basic Books, 2003, p. 213.

11   **"At some time in the future"**: conversation with Aubrey de Grey, July 5, 2007.

11   **"predictably irrational"**: Dan Ariely, *Predictably Irrational: The Hidden Forces That Shape Our Decisions*, Harper, 2008.

11   **"Human goodness appears when we least expect it"**: Anne Colby and William Damon, *Some Do Care*, Free Press, 1992, p. 2.

12   **"We are softened"**: James Q. Wilson, *The Moral Sense*, Free Press, 1993, p. 50.

12   **"I have found little that is good"**: Sigmund Freud, quoted in Armand M. Nicholi, *The Question of God*, Free Press, 2003, p. 181.

12   **"in order to gratify"**: Samuel P. Oliner and Pearl M. Oliner, *The Altruistic Personality: Rescuers of Jews in Nazi Europe*, Free Press, 1988, p. x.

12   **"Evolution is a process"**: Neil Levy, *What Makes Us Moral: Crossing the Boundaries of Biology*, Oneworld Publications, 2004, p. 41.

13   **"unearthed the will"**: Frans de Waal, *Primates and Philosophers: How Morality Evolved*, Princeton University Press, 2006, p. 8.

13   **"It is of the highest importance"**: Sholem Asch, quoted in Oliner and Oliner, *The Altruistic Personality*, p. xx.

15   **"a group of cooperative altruists"**: Marc D. Hauser, *Moral Minds: How Nature Designed Our Universal Sense of Right and Wrong*, HarperCollins, 2006, p. 360.

15   **"The *arete* of a knife"**: Jonathan Haidt, *The Happiness Hypothesis: Finding Modern Truth in Ancient Wisdom*, Basic Books, 2006, p. 156.

PART ONE: THE LAUGH THAT PRECEDED PHILOSOPHY

Homo Duplex

24   **"The explosion is so brutal"**: Antonio Damasio, *Descartes' Error: Emotion, Reason, and the Human Brain*, G. P. Putnam, 1994, p. 4.

24   **"The equilibrium . . . between his intellectual faculty"**: Ibid., p. 8.

25   **When the hypothalamuses of rats**: Haidt, *The Happiness Hypothesis*, p. 11.

26   **"fade away like radio noise"**: Robert Lee Hotz, "Scientists Draw Link Between Morality and Brain's Wiring," *Wall Street Journal*, May 11, 2007, p. B1.

Mirrors in the Mind

28   **"a baby's protests"**: Frans de Waal, *Good Natured: The Origins of Right and Wrong in Humans and Other Animals*, Harvard University Press, 1996, p. 188.

29   **"It took us several years"**: Sandra Blakeslee, "Cells That Read Minds," *New York Times*, January 10, 2006, p. C3.

29   **the discovery of mirror neurons . . . may well turn out:** V. Ramachandran, "Mirror Neurons and the Brain in a Vat," *Edge*, January 10, 2006, available at http://www.edge.org.

29   **"Mirror neurons allow us to grasp"**: Blakeslee, "Cells That Read Minds."

30   **Mirror neurons map the identical information:** Daniel Goleman, *Social Intelligence*, Bantam, 2006, p. 42.

30   **"actually register the pain"**: Blakeslee, "Cells That Read Minds."

31   **"imitative violence in viewers"**: Marco Iacoboni, "The Mirror Neuron Revolution," *Scientific American*, July 1, 2008 (online).

Mother and Child

33   **"Repeated tens of thousands of times"**: Mary Sykes Wylie, "Mindsight," *Psychotherapy Networker*, September/October, 2004 (online).

34   **Not long before his death:** Ibid.

34   **"Through mirroring"**: Ibid.

34   **Having found a secure base:** John Bowlby, *A Secure Base: Clinical Applications of Attachment Theory,* Routledge, London, 1988.

35   **"There is a sensible way"**: Judith Rich Harris, *The Nurture Assumption,* Simon and Schuster, 1998, p. 79.

35   **"both the alpha and omega"**: William James, *The Principles of Psychology,* Henry Holt, 1918, p. 551.

Venus and Mars

38   **"Once he has achieved fertilization"**: Edward O. Wilson, *On Human Nature,* Harvard University Press, 1978, p. 125.

38   **"If a man were given total freedom"**: Ibid.

39   **"Men do not know"**: Carol Gilligan, *In a Different Voice,* Harvard University Press, 1982, p. 17.

40   **"The blind willingness"**: Ibid., p. 104.

41   **When the same thing happens:** Daniel Goleman, *Emotional Intelligence: Why It Can Matter More than IQ,* Bantam, 1995, p. 131.

42   **Swedish researchers did an interesting experiment:** Benedict Carey, "Standing in Someone Else's Shoes," *New York Times,* December 1, 2008, p. C5.

42   **In a similar study using whites and blacks:** Ibid.

Emotions

43   **Emotions are surges of affect:** Martha C. Nussbaum, "Morality and Emotions" in the ethics chapter of *Routledge Encyclopedia of Philosophy* CD-ROM, v. 10.

44   **"Love is like a fever"**: Stendhal quoted by Victor C. De Munck, *Romantic Love and Sexual Behavior,* Praeger, 1998, p. 77.

44   **"[different] from kindred non-moral emotions"**: Edward Westermarck quoted in Frans de Waal, *Primates and Philosophers: How Morality Evolved,* Princeton University Press, 2006. p. 20.

45   **"the other-condemning"**: Jonathan Haidt, "The Moral Emotions" in R. J. Davidson, K. R. Scherer, and H. H. Goldsmith, eds., *Handbook of Affective Sciences,* Oxford University Press, 2003, pp. 852–70.

45   **"It didn't matter if you were"**: Lynn Grodzki, "An Interview with Candace Pert: Approaching a Theory of Emotion," 1995, http://primal page.com/pert.htm (online).

46   **"It's only when [the emotion]"**: Ibid.

47   **Using his FACS:** Dacher Keltner, *Born to Be Good: The Science of a Meaningful Life,* Norton, 2009, p. 47.

47   **"At the airport"**: Paul Ekman interview in Mark Matousek, "Spiritual Energy," *O: The Oprah Magazine,* July 1, 2003, p. 62.

48   **"special quality"**: Daniel Goleman interview, Ibid.

49   **a famous long-term study:** Keltner, *Born to Be Good,* p. 113.

49   **In a deadlocked negotiation:** Ibid., p. 135.

49   **In divorce studies:** Ibid., p. 135.

51   **"Entities can be like a hologram":** Daniel Goleman, *Emotional Intelligence: Why It Can Matter More than IQ,* Bantam, 1995, p. 294.

51   **"man within the breast":** Adam Smith, *The Theory of Moral Sentiments* (originally published in 1759), www.adamsmith.org (online).

52   **"The imagination":** William Hazlitt, *The Collected Works of William Hazlitt,* J. M. Dent and Company, 1903, p. 385.

53   **"the tyranny of the here and now":** Charles Tilly, "The Tyranny of the Here and Now," *Sociological Forum,* Springer, 1986, p. 179.

53   **"end up as juvenile delinquents":** Marc D. Hauser, *Moral Minds: How Nature Designed Our Universal Sense of Right and Wrong,* HarperCollins, 2006, p. 215.

53   **Children . . . better able to:** Ibid., p. 216.

55   **"But don't you see?":** Barbara Oakley, *Evil Genes: Why Rome Fell, Hitler Rose, Enron Failed, and My Sister Stole My Mother's Boyfriend,* Prometheus Books, 2007, p. 204.

56   **"the emotion of shame":** Michael Kimmel, *Guyland: The Perilous World Where Boys Become Men,* HarperCollins, 2008, p. 64.

56   **"proportional to the perceived importance":** Richard Joyce, *The Evolution of Morality,* MIT Press, 2006, p. 103.

57   **"fail safes like blushing":** Frans de Waal, *Good Natured: The Origins of Right and Wrong in Humans and Other Animals,* Harvard University Press, 1996, p. 108.

58   **seven different kinds of human aggression:** E. O. Wilson, *On Human Nature,* Harvard University Press, 1978, p. 101.

58   **physicians who tested high:** Goleman, *Emotional Intelligence,* p. 170.

59   **"War has been far too important":** Richard B. Lee, *Man the Hunter,* Aldine, 1969, p. 299.

59   **One of three sacred substances:** Erich Fromm, *The Anatomy of Human Destructiveness,* Henry Holt, 1973, p. 300.

60   **"The human body bristles":** "The Nature of Evil" (no author), Time.com, February 15, 1963 (online).

61   **"I suspect that if":** Edward O. Wilson, *On Human Nature,* p. 104.

63   **"The attempt to link love to God":** Jonathan Haidt, *The Happiness Hypothesis: Finding Modern Truth in Ancient Wisdom,* Basic Books, 2006, p. 132.

64   **If the previous owner is believed:** Ibid.

65   **"The law only forbids":** Edward Westermarck quoted in James George Fraser, *Totem and Exogamy,* Macmillan and Co., 1937, p. 97.

66   **Individuals with high:** Dacher Keltner, *Born to Be Good,* W. W. Norton, 2009, p. 243.

67 **"[The] new ardor which burns"**: William James, *The Varieties of Religious Experience*, Seven Treasures, 2009, p. 152.

67 **The *Oprah*-watching moms**: Haidt, *The Happiness Hypothesis*, p. 197.

68 **"Powerful moments of elevation"**: Jonathan Haidt quoted in Emily Yoffe, "Obama in Your Heart," *Slate*, December 3, 2008.

68 **"By stopping people"**: Haidt, *The Happiness Hypothesis*, p. 203.

Emotional Intelligence

70 **"We catch each other's emotions"**: Daniel Goleman in Mark Matousek, "We're Wired to Connect," *AARP Magazine*, January 2007 (online).

74 **In face-to-face interactions:** Stephen Nowicki and Marshall P. Duke, *Helping the Child Who Doesn't Fit In*, Peachtree Publications, 1992, p. 7.

74 **"The story of evil in the world"**: Lance Morrow, *Evil: An Investigation*, Basic Books, 2003, p. 56.

PART TWO: SUCKERS, GRUDGERS, AND CHEATERS

We Tell Ourselves Stories

81 **"language evolved as a replacement for physical grooming"**: Jonathan Haidt, *The Happiness Hypothesis: Finding Modern Truth in Ancient Wisdom*, Basic Books, 2006, p. 53.

81 **our first line of defense:** Ibid., p. 52.

81 **"Gossip paired with reciprocity"**: Ibid., p. 55.

82 **"a runaway competition"**: Edward O. Wilson, *On Human Nature*, Harvard University Press, 1978, p. 85.

82 **"There is an endless flow"**: Richard B. Lee, "The Kung Bushmen of Botswana," in M. G. Bicchieri (ed.), *Hunters and Gatherers Today*, Holt Rinehart and Winston, 1972, p. 327.

84 **"In our condemnation of others' hypocrisy"**: Haidt, *The Happiness Hypothesis*, p. 60.

84 **A landmark study:** Joanne Intrator and Robert Hare, *Journal of the Society of Biological Psychiatry* 42, no. 2, p. 96.

84 **"as if knowing the words but not the music"**: John Seabrook, "Suffering Souls," *New Yorker*, November 10, 2008 (online).

85 **"If every time"**: Josie Glausiusz, interview with Marc Hauser, "Is Morality Hardwired in Our DNA?" *Discover*, April 15, 2007, p. 62.

85 **"our minds construct"**: Richard G. Tedeschi, Crystal L. Park, and Lawrence Calhoun, *Post Traumatic Growth: Positive Changes in the Aftermath of Crisis*, Lawrence Erlbaum Associates, 1998, p. 287.

Who Am I?

88   **"Wow, what a strange and amazing thing"**: Jill Bolte Taylor, *My Stroke of Insight,* Viking, 2008, p. 42.

91   **"reflective, coherent, and emotionally rich"**: Mary Sykes Wylie, "Mindsight" *Psychotherapy Networker,* September/October, 2004 (online).

"Ought" Does Not Exist in Nature

93   **"To dislike something"**: Richard Joyce, *The Evolution of Morality,* MIT Press, 2006, p. 132.

94   **" 'Tis a common observation"**: David Hume, *A Treatise of Human Nature,* Longman Green, 1898, p. 167.

94   **"this quality of pitifulness"**: Ibid., p. 167.

94   **"no evidence that the human moral sensibility"**: Joyce, *Evolution of Morality,* p. 132.

95   **"growing a limb"**: Marc D. Hauser, *Moral Minds: How Nature Designed Our Universal Sense of Right and Wrong,* HarperCollins, 2006, p. xviii.

97   **"Our responses to threats"**: Jonathan Haidt, *The Happiness Hypothesis: Finding Modern Truth in Ancient Wisdom,* Basic Books, 2006, p. 60.

97   **In one test:** Ibid., p. 29.

97   **In marriage studies:** Ibid., p. 29.

When the Penis Gets Hard, the Brain Goes Soft

99   **"Unlike walking, eating, or hearing"**: Marc D. Hauser, *Moral Minds: How Nature Designed Our Universal Sense of Right and Wrong,* HarperCollins, 2006, p. 274.

100   **"An ape that in any circumstances"**: Richard Joyce, *Evolution of Morality,* MIT Press, 2006, p. 110.

100   **In a famous series of experiments:** Jonathan Haidt, "The Emotional Dog and Its Rational Tail: A Social Intuitionist Appeal to Moral Judgment," *Psychology Review,* no. 108 (2001), 814–34.

102   **"the press secretary for a secretive administration"**: Tamler Sommers, "Morally Dumbfounded: An Interview with Jonathan Haidt," *Believer,* August 2005 (online).

102   **Sex studies with teenagers:** Dan Ariely, *Predictably Irrational: The Hidden Forces that Shape Our Decisions,* Harper, 2008, pp. 96–97.

103   **the trolley problem presents:** Judith Jarvis Thompson, "Killing, Letting Die, and the Trolley Problem," *Monist* 59 (1976), p. 204.

104   **"I did not shoot"**: George Orwell in Sonia Orwell and Ian Angus, eds., *My Country Right or Left,* Harcourt Brace and World, 1968, p. 254.

The Mardi Gras Effect

105   **In Connorsville, Wisconsin:** Dribbleglass.com (online).
106   **"Justice is at best":** Lance Morrow, *Evil: An Investigation,* Basic Books, 2003, p. 197.
106   **"The rules of equity":** David Hume, *An Inquiry Concerning the Principles of Morals,* A. Millar, 1751, p. 15.
107   **inflict a maximum electrical shock:** Stanley Milgram, "Behavioral Study of Obedience," *Journal of Abnormal and Social Psychology* 67 (1963): 371–78.
108   **"We are *where* we live":** Philip Zimbardo, *The Lucifer Effect,* Random House, 2007, p. 321.
108   **"many traits that may be desirable":** Paul Babiak and Robert Hare quoted by John Seabrook, "Suffering Souls," *The New Yorker,* November 10, 2008 (online).
109   **four methods of compartmentalization:** Zimbardo, *The Lucifer Effect,* pp. 310–11.
110   **"He looked in astonishment":** William Golding, *The Lord of the Flies,* Faber and Faber, 1954, p. 83.
110   **"Dionysius's dominion includes":** Zimbardo, *The Lucifer Effect,* p. 306.
111   **a "good husband can . . . be":** Ibid., p. 214.

Suckers, Grudgers, and Cheaters

114   **But even when:** Dan Ariely, *Predictably Irrational: The Hidden Forces that Shape Our Decisions,* Harper, 2008, p. 201.
115   **payoff for finding the violation:** Jesse J. Prinz, *The Emotional Construction of Morals,* Oxford University Press, 2007, p. 249.
115   **Studies show that our brains respond differently:** Alan Sanfey, "Social Decision-Making: Insights from Game Theory and Neuroscience," *Science* 318 (October 2007): 598–602.
116   **"If that beggar is a member":** Shelly Kagan, *The Limits of Morality,* Clarendon Press, 1989, p. 102.
117   **Christmas cards:** Daniel Goleman, "What's Under the Tree? Clues to a Relationship," *New York Times,* December 19, 1989, p. C1.
117   **"The higher an animal has risen":** Erich Fromm, *The Anatomy of Human Destructiveness,* Henry Holt, 1973, p. 251.

The Green-Eyed Monsters

120   **"This culture feeds off an anxiety":** Andrew Harvey and Mark Matousek, *Dialogues with a Modern Mystic,* Quest, 1994, p. 33.
120   **"You could stare":** Mark Matousek, *When You're Falling, Dive: Lessons in the Art of Living,* Bloomsbury, 2008, p. 196.

121   **Today's average American child:** Bill McKibben, *Deep Economy,* Times Books, 2007, p. 4.

121   **2007 UNICEF study:** Russell Shorto, "Going Dutch," *New York Times Magazine,* May 3, 2009, p. 47.

121   **Liu Xian story:** Bill McKibben, *Deep Economy,* p. 41.

122   **"It is more rewarding":** Will Oldham quoted by Kelefa Sanneh in "The Pretender," *The New Yorker,* January 5, 2009 (online).

122   **"Envy is the great leveler":** Janice Brown, *The Seven Deadly Sins in the Work of Dorothy L. Sayers,* Kent State University Press, 1998, p. 37.

122   **"Central to the emotion of envy":** Joseph Epstein, *Envy,* Oxford University Press, 2003, p. 5.

122   **"motivating achievement, serving the conscience":** Marc D. Hauser, *Moral Minds: How Nature Designed Our Universal Sense of Right and Wrong,* HarperCollins, 2006, p. 282.

123   **"The infliction of cruelty":** Bertrand Russell, "On the Value of Scepticism" (essay) in *The Will to Doubt,* www.positiveatheism.org (online).

123   **"Men would watch":** Colin Turnbull, *The Mountain People,* Touchstone, 1972, p. 112.

123   **"[We] who lived in the concentration camps":** Viktor E. Frankl, *Man's Search for Meaning,* Pocket Books, 1959, p. 104.

Lex Talionis

125   **men enjoy retribution:** Ronald Bailey, "Morality on the Brain," *Reason,* January 27, 2006 (online).

125   **"Waving the bloody shirt":** Lance Morrow, *Evil: An Investigation,* Basic Books, 2003, p. 64.

125   **"Permissible evil is the evil we can live with":** Ibid., p. 149.

126   **"When punishment does not":** Alvin Goldman, quoted in Marc D. Hauser, *Moral Minds: How Nature Designed Our Universal Sense of Right and Wrong,* HarperCollins, 2006, p. 107.

129   **rated a smiling face:** Gilbert Harman, *The Nature of Morality,* Oxford University Press, 1977, p. 69.

129   **returned to terrorist activity:** Robert Mackey, The Lede Blog, *The New York Times,* May 28, 2009 (online).

Ends and Means

130   **"the psychology of the victim":** Lance Morrow, *Evil: An Investigation,* Basic Books, 2003, p. 156.

131   **in a study of people:** C. Daniel, Gregory Batson, Elizabeth Collins, and Adam A. Powell, "Doing Business After the Fall: The Virtue of Moral Hypocrisy," *Journal of Business Ethics* 66, no. 4 (July 2006) (online).

132 **maturing levels of ethical awareness:** Adapted from the Heinz dilemma. See Lawrence Kohlberg, *Essays on Moral Development,* vol. 1., Harper and Row, 1981, p. 59.

133 **"Some forms of merely risking":** Shelly Kagan, *Limits of Morality,* Clarendon Press, 1989, p. 87.

Game Theory

136 **Once resistant polluters:** "25 Big Companies that Are Going Green," *Business Pundit,* July 29, 2008 (online).

137 **"In the same way that humans enjoy sex":** Adam Smith, quoted by Diane Ravitch, *The English Reader,* Oxford University Press, 2006, p. 115.

137 **"Every individual necessarily":** Adam Smith, *The Wealth of Nations* (published in 1776), adamsmith.org (online).

137 **"moving against people":** Karen Horney, *Our Inner Conflicts: A Constructive Theory of Neurosis,* W. W. Norton and Co., New York, 1945, p. 63.

Altruism

140 **people who perform altruistic acts *without* an emotional basis:** Wikipedia, "Reciprocal Altruism."

141 **"Those agents who most effectively":** Reinhold Niebuhr, quoted in Gene Outka, *Agape,* Yale University Press, 1972, p. 31.

141 **reformers and helpers:** Anne Colby and William Damon, *Some Do Care,* Free Press, 1992, p. 277.

142 **"by physically removing oneself from the problem":** Samuel P. Oliner and Pearl M. Oliner, *The Altruistic Personality: Rescuers of Jews in Nazi Europe,* Free Press, 1988, p. 174.

142 **"We learn by early inductive reasoning":** Ibid., p. 179.

144 **"The hero and the saint":** Mihaly Csikszentmihalyi, *Flow: The Psychology of Optimal Experience,* Harper and Row, 1990, p. 218.

PART THREE: MAN IS WOLF TO MAN

Loyalty

148 **"Man defending his honor":** Nathan Glazer and Daniel P. Moynihan, eds., *Ethnicity,* Harvard University Press, 1975, p. 92.

Us Versus Them

152 **"Human beings are consistent":** Edward O. Wilson, *On Human Nature,* Harvard University Press, 1978, p. 163.

153 **"The Flemish have Walloon jokes":** Lance Morrow, *Evil: An Investigation,* Basic Books, 2003, p. 25.

155   "**Should one of *them* presume**": Daniel Goleman, *Social Intelligence,* Bantam, 2006, p. 299.

155   "**With the words us-them**": Martin Buber, *I and Thou,* Simon and Schuster, 1971, p. 13.

155   "**Humankind's noblest achievement**": Frans de Waal, *Primates and Philosophers: How Morality Evolved,* Princeton University Press, 2006, p. 55.

156   "**a species or a population within a species**": Richard Dawkins, *The Selfish Gene,* Oxford University Press, 1989, p. 7.

156   **mutual trust . . . between different racial groups:** Benedict Carey, "Tolerance over Race Can Spread, Studies Find," *New York Times,* November 6, 2009, p. A20.

Group Narcissism

157   "**in which only the [narcissist] himself**": Erich Fromm, *The Anatomy of Human Destructiveness,* Henry Holt, 1973, p. 227.

158   "**An individual, unless he is mentally very sick**": Ibid., p. 255.

158   "**the Chinese knew the narcissistic joy**": Alain Peyrifitte quoted in Sam Vaknin, "Narcissists, Group Behavior, and Terrorism," *Global Politician,* August 8, 2005 (online).

159   **a startling 41 percent:** Philip Zimbardo, *The Lucifer Effect,* Random House, 2007, p. 265.

159   "**We like to think**": Gregory Berns quoted in Sandra Blakeslee, "What Other People Say May Change What We See," *New York Times,* June 28, 2005 (online).

160   "**privileged insight into**": Sam Vaknin, "Narcissists, Group Behavior, and Terrorism," *Global Politician,* August 8, 2005 (online).

160   a "**gap between reality and grandiose fantasies**": Ibid.

161   "**It is always possible to bind together**": Sigmund Freud, *Civilization and Its Discontents,* Norton, 1962, p. 114.

161   "**We must be honest**": Heinrich Himmler, Speech to the Meeting of SS Majors at Posen," *Nazi Conspiracy and Aggression,* vol. IV, USGPO, Washington, 1946 (online).

Memes

162   "**the meme complexes**": Richard Dawkins, *The Selfish Gene,* Oxford University Press, 1989, p. 199.

164   "**Saying with our actions**": Joseph Goldstein, *One Dharma: The Emerging Western Buddhism,* HarperCollins, 2003, p. 78.

165   "**When the minority's behavior**": Anne Colby and William Damon, *Some Do Care,* Free Press, 1992, p. 23.

165 **"outstanding personalities who embodied"**: Erich Fromm, *The Anatomy of Human Destructiveness*, Henry Holt, 1973, p. 297.

166 **"The meme for blind faith"**: Dawkins, *The Selfish Gene*, p. 195.

166 **"If a man believes in a different god"**: Ibid., p. 198.

166 **Mennonite and Amish children:** Richard Joyce, *The Evolution of Morality*, MIT Press, 2006, p. 129.

000 **"Even if the map"**: Fromm, *The Anatomy of Human Destructiveness*, p. 259.

Donkeys and Elephants

169 **"[Systems] which have existed"**: Jonathan Haidt and Jesse Graham, "When Morality Opposes Justice: Conservatives Have Moral Intuitions that Liberals May Not Recognize," *Social Justice Research* 20, no. 1 (October 18, 2006) (online).

169 **"Populations with long crowding histories"**: Frans de Waal, *Good Natured: The Origins of Right and Wrong in Humans and Other Animals*, Harvard University Press, 1966, p. 200.

170 **Areas with less mobility:** Haidt and Graham: "When Morality Opposes Justice: Conservatives Have Moral Intuitions that Liberals May Not Recognize," *Social Justice Research*, February 1, 2006 (online).

170 **"protect the zone of discretionary choice"**: Ibid.

170 **"ethical life takes as its starting point"**: Jonathan Haidt, *The Happiness Hypothesis: Finding Modern Truth in Ancient Wisdom*, Basic Books, 2006, p. 188.

172 **"can't just dismiss this stuff"**: Jonathan Haidt, TED Conference address, December 10, 2008., www.ted.com/talks/jonathan_haidt_on_the_moral_mind.html.

PART FOUR: THE HIGHER A MONKEY CLIMBS

Holy Shit

177 **"a mass lethal poisoning"**: Gilliam Flaccus, "Oregon Town Never Recovered from Scare," Associated Press, October 19, 2001.

179 **"We may not be"**: Iris Makler, "Nature of Evil," Australian Broadcasting System, February 1, 2006 (online).

The Dark Triad

180 **"the dark triad"**: Delroy L. Paulhus and Kevin M. Williams, "The Dark Triad of Personality: Narcissism, Machiavellianism, and Psychopathy," *Journal of Research in Personality*, vol. 36, no. 6 (December 2002) p. 556.

182 **"They felt sorry for themselves"**: Lance Morrow, *Evil: An Investigation,* Basic Books, 2003, p. 60.

183 **"They are, in fact, the two poles of the false self"**: Mark Epstein, *Thoughts Without a Thinker: Psychotherapy from a Buddhist Perspective,* Basic Books, 1995, p. 64.

185 **"Where would we be today"**: Barbara Oakley, *Evil Genes: Why Rome Fell, Hitler Rose, Enron Failed and My Sister Stole My Mother's Boyfriend,* Prometheus Books, 2007, p. 292.

185 **"At eighteen months"**: Ibid., p. 102.

186 **The psychopathy checklist**: Robert D. Hare, "Psychopathy as a Risk Factor for Violence," *Psychiatric Quarterly* 70, no. 3 (March 1999) (online).

186 **Psychopaths about to receive an electrical shock**: Daniel Goleman, *Social Intelligence,* Bantam, 2006, p. 110.

186 **"The presence of a potential victim"**: Marc D. Hauser, *Moral Minds: How Nature Designed Our Universal Sense of Right and Wrong,* HarperCollins, 2006, p. 233.

187 **"The whole world is pining for light"**: Merwan Sheriar Irani (Meher Baba), *Beams from Meher Baba on the Spiritual Panorama,* Sheriar Books, 1958, p. 49.

187 **"To torture oneself or to torture others"**: Bhagwan Rajneesh, "Ecstasy: The Forgotten Language" (public talk), December 11, 1976 (online).

Evil

189 **"Male Kodiak bears"**: Lance Morrow, *Evil: An Investigation,* Basic Books, 2003, p. 32.

190 **"Some Serb men"**: Ibid., p. 64.

191 **"If only there were evil"**: Aleksandr I. Solzhenitsyn, *The Gulag Archipelago: 1918–1956,* Harper & Row, 1973, vol. 1, p. 168.

191 **But the most destructive**: Morrow, *Evil: An Investigation,* p. 106.

194 **"Possessing an excessive carbon footprint"**: Michael Specter, "Big Foot," *The New Yorker,* February 25, 2008 (online).

196 **"Generosity and modesty"**: Erich Fromm, *The Anatomy of Human Destructiveness,* Henry Holt, 1973, p. 163.

197 **"there is goodness entangled"**: Samuel P. Oliner and Pearl M. Oliner, *The Altruistic Personality: Rescuers of Jews in Nazi Europe,* Free Press, 1988, p. xii.

Playing with Power

199 **"Man recognized that he could use"**: Erich Fromm, *The Anatomy of Human Destructiveness,* Henry Holt, 1973, p. 188.

200 **"There is a great difference"**: Ibid., p. 186.

201 **The more division of labor**: Ibid., p. 174.

201 **"No longer the womb"**: Ibid., p. 189.

One Up, One Down

203   "**takes the group**": Jonathan Haidt, "Moral Psychology and the Misun-
derstanding of Religion," *Edge*, September 22, 2007 (online).

205   "**Two children pretending that a stick**": Michael Tomasello, "How Are
Humans Unique?" *New York Times Magazine*, May 25, 2008 (online).

The Passions

208   "**The truth is**": Erich Fromm, *The Anatomy of Human Destructiveness*,
Henry Holt, 1973, p. 31.

209   "**Life turning against itself**": Ibid., p. 31.

209   "**Man cannot live**": Ibid., p. 29.

PART FIVE: HOW OUGHT I TO LIVE?

The Holy Question

221   **made a surprising request:** Pumla Godobo-Madikizela, *A Human Being
Died That Night,* Houghton Mifflin, 2003, p. 4.

222   "**You must be strong**": Eva Eiger, quoted by Al Siebert in *The Survivor
Personality,* Perigee Books, 1996, p. 238.

224   **Studies of religious experience:** Jonathan Haidt, "The New Synthesis in
Moral Psychology," *Science,* May 18, 2007, p. 998.

224   "**Love is rejoicing**": H. Richard Niebuhr, quoted in Gene Outka, *Agape,*
Yale University Press, 1972, p. 9.

225   "**The spiritual life**": Frans de Waal, *Good Natured: The Origins of Right
and Wrong in Humans and Other Animals,* Harvard University Press, 1966,
p. 209.

226   **V. Ramachandran, the neurologist:** John Colapinto, "Ramachandran's
Mirror Trick," *The New Yorker,* May 6, 2009 (online).

228   "**The modern West is the first culture**": Mircea Eliade quoted in
Jonathan Haidt, *The Happiness Hypothesis: Finding Modern Truth in
Ancient Wisdom,* Basic Books, 2006, p. 193.

228   "**We've been Novocained to death**": Matthew Fox quoted by Mark
Matousek, *When You're Falling, Dive: Lessons in the Art of Living,*
Bloomsbury, 2008, p. 190.

229   "**The whole meaning of sin**": Joseph Le Conte, *Evolution: Its Nature, Its
Evidences and Its Relation to Religious Thought,* D. Appleton and Company, Boston, 1888, p. 330.

230   "**What is termed Sin**": Oscar Wilde, *Intentions,* Project Gutenberg, 1997
(online).

230   "**Mind is the forerunner of all things**": Joseph Goldstein, *One
Dharma: The Emerging Western Buddhism,* HarperCollins, 2003, p. 97.

Acknowledgments

The author wishes to thank the following people for their generous help with this book: Phyllis Grann, Joy Harris, Jackie Montalvo, Amanda Romeo, Robert Levithan, Barbara Graham, Florence Falk, Marcia Lippman, Nina Wise, Emily Benedek, Eve Ensler. And to David Moore for his wit—and patience.